The Elephant in the Classroom

How Our Fear of the Truth Hurts Kids and How Every Student Can Succeed

Mack R. Hicks Ph.D.

Copyright @ 2014 by Mack R Hicks, PhD

All rights reserved. No portion of this book may be reproduced or transmitted in any form whatsoever, including electronic, mechanical, or any information storage or retrieval system, except as may be expressly permitted in 1976 copyright act, or in writing from the publisher. Requests for permission should be addressed to:
Splenium House Publishers, LLC
6710 86th Avenue N.
Pinellas Park, Florida, 33782

Hicks, Mack R.
The Elephant in the Classroom (How Our Fear of the Truth Hurts Kids and How Every Student Can Succeed).
Cover design and interior design: Create Space, Inc.

Copyright @2014 Mack Hicks
All rights reserved
ISBN: 0971258708
ISBN- 978-0-9712587-0-9
Library of Congress Control Number: 2014916642
Splenium House Publishers, LLC
Pinellas Park, Florida
Manufactured in the USA

Dedication

A SALUTE TO OUR HARDWORKING PUBLIC SCHOOL TEACHERS, ADMINISTRATORS, AND SCHOOL BOARD MEMBERS, WHO ARE ASKED TO DO A DIFFICULT IF NOT IMPOSSIBLE JOB.

Acknowledgements

Many generous people took time to look over these pages and give me feedback on concept, writing, and organization. My deepest thanks and appreciation to all of you.

The following persons gave me the courtesy of their time as well as much needed background information: Terry Boehm, Jeff Eversole, Frank Fuller, John Leones, and Jon and Betsy Reynolds,

A special thanks to neuropsychologist Andy Hicks, PhD, CEO of Center Academy Schools, who supplied much psychological and educational insight and who helped analyze research data and statistics. His input formed the basis of many of the questions and solutions put forth in this book.

Steve Keteltas brought rigorous line editing, poetic insight and critical analysis to this book. Thanks, Steve.

Readers and constructive critics gave me valuable feedback and insight: Margaret Dawson, Stephanie Graham, Eric Larson, Ph.D. and Sheri Watson. Doug Hicks shared some critical right-brain reactions. Professor Philip Hicks, Ph.D. did not spare the rod when he offered helpful criticism. I think he gave me a poor grade but his professor's eye helped turn the book around.

Jim and Sharon Moorhead (Moorhead, Inc.) gave me valuable feedback and helped me with *Psychology Today Magazine* web articles so that I could concentrate on "the Elephant."

Susan Hicks was the number one researcher, digging up pertinent news and journal articles hither and yon.

I am grateful to all of you. The Elephant thanks you. Emily and Jaylen thank you. I thank you.

Author's Note

This book is based on the experiences of the author and reflects his perception of the past, present and future. The personalities, events, actions and conversations portrayed within this text have been taken from memories, interviews, research studies, letters, personal papers and media-related articles and features. *The Elephant in the Classroom* is based on extensive personal interviews, research and insights from the author. Certain names have been changed and recognizable characteristics disguised except for those of contributing experts.

Table of Contents

Acknowledgements: v
Author's Note vii

    Introduction: Blindsided 1

1. How Selection and "Creaming" Creates "Killing Fields." 7

2. The Solution: The Elephant-in-the-Classroom Plan 17

3. The First Great Myth: All Children have
   the Same Academic Potential. 30

4. The Second Great Myth: All Kids are Pretty Much the Same 47

5. The Third Great Myth: All Kids Should go to College 59

6. Crisis in American Education 69

7. *Magic:* How Seeing the Elephant Changes Everything 76

8. What about other Opinions and Reforms? 80

9. How the Elephant's Plan Changes Things 98

10. Marketing the Elephant 105

11. What will the Elephant's Plan Cost? 110

12. Why Do We Refuse to See the Elephant? 116

   To Contact the Author 125

Appendix 1   Crisis in American Education 127

Appendix 2   Career Offerings. 133

Appendix 3   The Career Test. 135

Appendix 4   The College Test. 137

Appendix 5   Non-College Grads 139

Appendix 6   Help Your Child — Now! 141

   About the Author 145

Introduction
Blindsided.

The kids who wanted to be somebody. This is the story of a girl named Emily and her friend Jaylen. It's a story that begins in school classrooms all across our country. What happens there often leads to discouragement, unhappiness, and an unfulfilled life. Emily (not her real name) is a "good girl." Good, because of her strength, integrity, and emotional warmth. She didn't know her father, but her mother sometimes showed her pictures of a man with a broken body playing a piano in a dingy barroom. Her mother also kept the Purple Heart he had received in the Afghanistan war. She told Emily that her father was *somebody*. Emily always wanted to be somebody too — just like her father.

Emily started school with a smile on her face. Teachers at her church-school liked her, and she did well in public kindergarten and first grade. But she had reading problems in the second grade, and her smile started to fade. Emily tried to pay attention, obeyed her teachers' rules, and studied harder than most of the kids in her class. Her mother wanted more than anything for Emily to attend college, because no one in the family had made it that far.

Emily kept plugging away in elementary school, spending two hours studying every day, even on Saturdays. Her mother helped her with reading when she got time off from her job as a waitress. Emily managed to attain a 2.5 grade point average, but when she encountered classes in biology and chemistry in middle school, her grades plummeted. World history wasn't easy, either.

Nice counselor.
The counselor at her school suggested that Emily might enjoy some career options such as studying to be a veterinarian's assistant or an assistant nurse working in a hospital. This excited Emily because she loved animals and enjoyed babysitting for the little girls down the street. She hoped she could get good grades again — and be somebody. Her mother was unsure about career studies, because she was set on Julie going to college but knew Emily was unhappy. Perhaps these courses would put that beautiful smile back on her face. Emily could think about college later.

Emily signed up for the veterinarian and nursing courses, but then something unfortunate happened. Emily and her mother were informed that Emily's academic grades weren't high enough for acceptance into the career programs. That didn't make sense to Emily and her mother, but the counselor said it was a state law and Emily would need to improve her grades and pass the world history exam before she would have sufficient time to take career courses. Emily had failed the world history test five times and just couldn't seem to remember the dates and events from so long ago.

When Emily was in the 11th grade, the counselor discovered a new program that would accept her, even if she couldn't pass the world history exam. This career program was part-time at another school across town and that school would be happy to give her a chance. Emily was excited and her mother saw an immediate, positive change in her personality. The school system did not provide transportation to the new program, however, and Emily's mother couldn't afford a car, so Emily couldn't go. She kept trying and studied even harder but still got poor grades. Emily eventually gave up and dropped out of school. She found someone who thought she was special and became pregnant.

Without hope.
Emily is still a "good girl," only now she's a young adult without much hope for the future and is a burden to society. Emily's story is not unique. She represents the *majority* of school children in our public schools. You see, Emily was never cut out for college. Her mother didn't read to her as a young child and

she didn't like academics. Emily's working memory was poor and she suffered from a short attention span.

We are facing enormous problems in this country. The purpose of this book is to expose a great American myth and help us find the elephant in the classroom. *The myth is that all Americans are equal in terms of talent and skills.* The best thing about this myth is that it represents a great American Dream. In America, anyone can make it to the top with sacrifice and hard work.

Yes, we Americans are a nervy lot. We can pull ourselves up by our own bootstraps. In this way, it's a good myth. A myth that gives us hope. A myth that makes us proud. Who says everyone can't be a Harvard PhD? Who says everyone can't be an astronaut? Who says everyone can't win the Nobel Peace Prize? Who says everyone can't win a gold medal at the Olympics? *And who says not everyone should go to college?*

I do.

And once most Americans think this through, they will agree that the odds of accomplishing any of these things are pretty daunting, including college, or at least *real* colleges that haven't lowered their standards. The universal desire to reach the summit of a college education reminds me of General George Pickett's infantry charge at Gettysburg, an action that hastened the end of the United States Civil War. Amassing troops and sending them up a hill into murderous gunfire, without a special plan, led to horrendous casualties. Yes, the Confederate general, Robert E. Lee, was the war's greatest tactician, but he made a tragic mistake at Gettysburg.

And what about Emily's friend, Jaylen (not his real name)? Should he have attended college? His parents and teachers thought so. Jaylen earned high scores on achievement tests and carried a 4.0 grade average into his senior year in high school. This sounded well and good, but when the *average* grade for all students was 3.6, and student grades didn't rank him against classmates, and achievement tests didn't compare him to national norms, it was difficult to know just where he stood academically.

Not all of his classes were challenging either, and he shared several classes with Emily, who he occasionally helped with her homework. He wanted to please his parents, who had not attended college, and he knew they were hurt and disappointed when Jaylen's older brother dropped out of school.

As it turns out, Jaylen had all four of the elephant's sturdy legs that are necessary for college: *academic ability, motivation, self-control, and the ability to focus.* He was vice-president of the student council and was named to the National Honor Society. His grades and honors led him to an academic scholarship at a small liberal arts college.

But when he got to college that fall, something shocking happened. Jaylen was told that he lacked basic skills in writing and mathematics. As a result, counselors enrolled him in remedial classes. Jaylen's parents were dismayed. An honors student needed special help? This created additional financial burdens for his parents, and it took Jaylen five years to graduate from college.

How would recognizing the elephant change things? Students such as Jaylen, who are capable of abstract academic learning, would operate in a much more challenging and competitive environment, leading to satisfactory college preparation without leaving their neighborhood school. Students such as Emily would begin full-time career courses in middle school or high school without concern about high-stakes state or federal achievement testing. They would study and train in a rich, creative environment where they would earn occupational certificates, nationally-recognized industry certifications, and apprenticeships. Career training that would lead to well-paying positions in the workforce.

This realization would also affect other areas such as dropout rates, school testing, bullying, and behavior problems, etc.

Those who ignore the elephant do so at their own peril. This is especially true of our elephant. While she seems destined to breaking up furniture, she'd really like to get out of the room and help us out. She is closest to the action and she may give us advice from time-to-time.

Without including this reality in any formulation of education and learning, we distort our perception of what is true, real, and important. We must render the elephant visible in order to rescue Emily, Jaylen, and other vulnerable students; young Americans with hopes and dreams and special talents.

That is what this book seeks to do. And believe it or not, we're not going to blame the teachers. And we're not going to blame the teachers' union, or the curriculum. We're not even going to blame the parents.

Hmm. Who's left?

one

How Selection and "Creaming" Creates "Killing Fields."

The formula.
This formula explains all we need to know about identifying the causes underlying the crisis in American schools today:

If SC ≥ 50%

Then NSC = (BC+ HT+ MA) − (AC + AA) = CCAS

Let's take a look at the causes underlying our educational problems before returning to this formula.

Creaming.
Why do we treat Emily and Jalen in such an unfair way, you might be wondering. Before I suggest a way to help Emily and Jaylen, let's remove the eye mask and look at the real parade ground, where our elephant does her stuff. What kind of a place is this, and how did it evolve? Is this a diabolical system created to frustrate kids? No, but unfortunately it doesn't work in the best interests of our young students.

Most of us believe that all children ages 4 through 18 are in neighborhood public schools or schools reachable by bus. They see this school as a neat and tidy box where children are taught the 3Rs plus lots of content material such as history, foreign languages, and social studies. But believe me, that's not the way it is.

A true analysis of our public schools, according to the elephant, shows us that students in the top 30% on achievement tests, who are also motivated, are excellent candidates for rigorous college-prep courses, but are instead taking some advanced courses along with many non-challenging courses. Why?

Blended classes.
Students are taking pretty much the same vanilla courses because of the myth that everyone is the same and the parents' desire to have their children attend college, even if their kids are not motivated and do not have the academic ability and/or willpower to succeed in college. As a result, this frustrates students such as Jaylen, whose best fit is college. It also frustrates students such as Emily, who are not going to complete college and will benefit most from performance-based career training that results in skills leading to employment and a successful career.

Students in the top 30% on academic achievement tests have also lost a number of their fellow academic achievers to other private and public school programs. In a school with a hypothetical 1000 students, we would have expected approximately 250 students who are both capable of, and motivated for, college-prep work. But of those 250 students, I would estimate that 70% (175) of this academically select group have enrolled in *schools of choice* inside or outside the public system. This leaves us with 75 students with high academic potential or 9 % of that school's refigured population of 825.

Where did they go?
Where are these choice schools? Some 10% percent of school-aged students are not in the neighborhood school because they are in private-religious, private-secular, or home-based schools. These students may not all be above average in academic ability, but they often have at least three of the elephant's legs: ability to focus, motivation, and self-control.

Another 8% of all students are not in this school because they are in private voucher-supported schools or charter schools. A voucher program gives vouchers to parents to use to pay for private school tuition. Charter schools are part of the public system, but are operated privately. (A charter school is much like one large voucher, but that voucher goes to an entire school rather than to individual parents). Attendance at these private-voucher and private-public charter schools requires vigilance on the part of parents. They need to know which schools are available and need to be motivated to find the best programs for their children. This leads to *selected* students and typically more cooperative parents.

Public schools oppose these programs and even oppose their own public charter schools, because they suspect these programs *cream off* the "best" parents and kids. (Local public schools are less opposed to learning-disabled students finding their way to charters or private schools, however, because these children are poor test-takers who lower public school test scores).

Another 7% are not in their neighborhood school because they are in public, magnet schools. These schools were developed in part to compete with private schools and offer specialty programs such as the arts and technology. Included in this group are the highly structured, so-called fundamental schools that require parents to sign a contract agreeing to a standard dress uniform and compliance with explicit rules.

General open enrollment that includes Advanced International Certificates (AICE), virtual instruction, International Baccalaureate, Lab Schools, etc., make up another 13%. (For more details, please see Appendix 2).

Meanwhile, back in the elephant jungle, something extraordinary is happening. We should have as many as 80% of our neighborhood school students in career and technical training. What do you think that percentage is in the state of Florida? *Five percent*! Yep, this group makes up only 161,000 students (State of Florida figures) or less than 5% of the 3.5 million students in Florida in 2012-13!

While some public schools and teachers' unions decry voucher and charter schools, their own increasing use of fundamental schools and magnet schools could be subject to the same criticism. Similar to a *magnet*, these schools *attract* high achieving kids and families from higher socio-economic levels, leaving the "regular," neighborhood school with fewer academically capable kids and fewer motivated parents. (These are the killing fields).

Coffee, anyone?
How to make triple cream coffee. How much cream do we like in our coffee? What are the factors that result in creaming off more academically capable students? *Selection* seems to be the key to creaming. There are two types of selective factors, subtle and overt:

Subtle selection:
1. A wealthy neighborhood draws higher-achieving students at the expense of schools in moderate and poor income areas. (Parents not residing in a wealthy neighborhood can, and do, give fictitious residency addresses or find courses available in the top schools that are not available in their local school, triggering automatic enrollment).
2. The opening of courses or schools that require parental vigilance will lead to creaming. An example is magnet schools.
3. Any programs or schools with waiting lists create a selective population. Examples would include charter schools and fundamental schools.
4. Programs requiring parent or student private transportation.
5. Having the best teachers and courses because of insider information.
6. The use of private tutors.
7. Having parents who are active in the school, such as room mothers or PTA (Parent-Teacher Association) members.

Overt selection:
1. Children in AP (advanced placement).
2. Children in gifted classes.
3. Children in gifted charter schools (These are public-private schools).
4. Children in the International Baccalaureate Programs.
5. Children admitted to college-prep courses based on achievement test scores. (Public school collegiate academies).

6. Children admitted to collegiate high schools that promise a high school degree and two years of college credits — all in only four years!

Is creaming bad? Not when it's an overt and transparent selective placement based on ability, motivation, and unique personality factors and interests. *But the needs of all students should be addressed.* Emily and Jaylen fall in the coffee grounds at the bottom of the hypothetical school coffee cup, but they deserve special programs as well.

Creaming leads to selective schools in wealthy neighborhoods, gifted charters, magnets, fundamental schools, schools with the International Baccalaureate, schools with collegiate prep, and selective career schools. These schools have much rich cream (above average state test scores) because their students do well on the state academic achievement tests. Let's call these the "Lake Wobegone Schools, where all students are above average" (With apologies to Garrison Keillor, *A Prairie Home Companion*).

Nonselective or regular neighborhood schools (skimmed-milk schools) result in below average state achievement test scores, yet teachers, principals and administrators at these schools are expected to show significant academic achievement and high graduation rates.

When these schools, which are filled with many students who are not high academic achievers and have little interest in abstract, verbal learning, are averaged into the school district's overall grade, I estimate that it pulls the grade point average down from a about a 4.0+ to a 3.6. (The grade point average for all students is 3.6). And we complain that we're not keeping up with Norway and China! Now, we are beginning to expose the elephant, but Alice *(in Wonderland)* is still combing her blonde locks, staring into the looking glass, and shaking her head in disbelief.

An example of the difference between selective and nonselective schools can be found in state achievement scores in one county in the state of Florida, May, 2014. It is easy to spot the differences in achievement. Five of the selective public schools report 74% to 85% of third-graders who test proficient in reading. Three nonselective schools hover around the 15th percentile. Other schools fall somewhere in between. EDUCATION MATTERS, FCAT: "A Closer Look," *Tampa Bay Times*, May 30, 2014.

Look in your own school district. You'll find the same thing.

And, based on the following data, it's apparent that almost half of the students in the State of Florida attend a school of their choosing, and this does not include parents who have selected their child's school through the process of choosing where to purchase a home, or falsifying their residency address.

This leaves a large number of students with only a limited opportunity to succeed. These are the non-selected, non-creamed kids who reside in the killing fields. So what's the bottom line? Because of creaming, we end up with a few neighborhood but *non*-inner-city high schools where 20% of students are sent home for at least one day for fighting and where 30% of students are absent 21+ days during the school year. Lisa Gartner, "Teacher's Call for Aid got a Busy signal," *Tampa Bay Times*, February 6, 2014. In 2011-12 in Pinellas County, Florida, there were 846 school-related arrests. Most of these were for misdemeanors, but these violations could result in an arrest record that could keep these youngsters from getting jobs for the rest of their lives. Lisa Gartner, "School Chief's Topic: Arrests," *Tampa Bay Times*, March 11, 2014.

I think these kids are trying to tell us something. They've gone A.W.O.L.! (*Absent Without Leave*).

Are we the dropouts?

Since we're having difficulty with this residue of students (the coffee grounds) who are not selected for other programs, maybe what we're really doing is using magnets, charters, and other programs, academic and career, to drop out of the killing fields. Yes, maybe we're the dropouts!

Since schools are not permitted to dismiss frustrated, unhappy, and unprepared students and parents, perhaps what we're doing today, as a society, is dropping out. But

THE FLORIDA PreK-12 EDUCATION LANDSCAPE:

1.5 million students choose

Parents long have chosen their child's school through where they decide to live, but Florida expands choice beyond the neighborhood by offering learning options that help students find the education that works best for them. In 2012-13, 1.5 million of the 3.5 million students in PreK-12 education — or 42 percent — attended a school of their choosing.

263,686 In Open Enrollment
Students in 52 of the state's 67 districts chose school through "open enrollment" plans.

242,737 In Private Schools
Students whose parents chose to pay for their education at one of 2,268 private schools.

219,027 In Choice and Magnet Programs
Students chose from fundamental, academic and special programs at 1,564 different schools.

203,240 In Charter Schools
Students attended 578 privately operated charter schools that are paid by school districts.

160,601 In Career and Professional Academies
Students pursue career and professional interests in programs at 511 different high schools.

144,414 In PreKindergarten Scholarships
Four-year-olds who attended VPK in private schools and centers across the state.

75,801 In Home Education
Students received their education at home while reporting results to the school district.

51,075 In Tax Credit Scholarships
Low-income students attended 1,338 different private schools.

29,872 In McKay Scholarships
Students with disabilities attended 1,163 different private schools.

16,363 In Advanced International Certificate of Education
Students enrolled in AICE programs in 11th and 12th grades.

13,997 In Fulltime Virtual Instruction
Students completed a fulltime program of virtual instruction.

13,224 In International Baccalaureate
Students enrolled in the intensive academic programs at 77 different schools.

10,932 In No Child Left Behind transfers
Students chose a different school because their assigned one didn't meet federal standards.

7,124 In Lab Schools
Students were enrolled in "laboratory schools" run by five different universities.

3,464 In Opportunity Scholarships
Students chose a different school because their assigned one didn't meet state standards.

= 1,455,557 students at schools of their choice

Source: 2012-13 Florida Department of Education data

we're dropping out to find a better place and leaving students such as Emily and Jaylen behind to face underachievement and unemployment.

Perhaps I'm being a little too critical, here. Rather than abandoning students and teachers in non-selective schools, perhaps we're just doing what is normal. *Striving for a better life for ourselves and our children.* We want to be effective workers and professionals. Parents want their children in the safest, most effective programs available. Good teachers want satisfying work and the chance to teach with other good teachers in a nurturing environment. They want cooperative parents and appreciative learners. Is that so bad?

Liberty and happiness.
Aren't these promises found in our constitution? The desire for liberation from the killing fields is normal and instinctual. I'm not proud to admit it, but I will run as fast as I can from any dysfunctional environment that effects my kids, especially when I know I can't change it.

Job skills and awareness of the employment culture are critical for less academically capable students such as Emily. But the same is true for a good number of academic strivers such as Jaylen who may flunk out of college or graduate with few employment skills.

We need to provide our youth with job skills and the lessons they teach. A school is an academic place; a place where academics are taught, but more than half our students need to learn job skills, not academic ones. We *pretend* to teach college academic skills to all of our students and our students *pretend* to learn academic skills for college. This is almost as bad as the situation in East Germany under Soviet occupation where the citizens said about the authorities, "they pretend to pay us what we need and we pretend to work."

If we look at the big picture, some students are receiving benefits in one way or another, and certainly there is nothing wrong with attending public school magnets or charter schools, but a higher percentage of students remaining in our theoretical schools need career programs — perhaps as many as 90% of the neighborhood school's *refigured* population.

You might be wondering if all of the kids who are left behind will benefit from career studies. Yes, they can, and they will benefit more from career programs than they do trying to learn facts and figures they will never use.

Why am I confident that they can succeed with career studies? At the present time, career programs are offered at two difficulty levels. The more challenging career certification programs provide rigorous preparation and thinking skills as well as math and science. These students receive high school and even college credits upon completion of these nationally-certified courses. The certificates are performance-based and certify the individual as competent to perform a specific skill.

Students who are below average in motivation, ability, or self-control, and who can't handle the rigor of these nationally-certified career programs will still find stimulation and motivation in "industry-search" certificates. These certificates involve more redundant and routine activities, but sometimes in complex environments. An example would be a nurse's aide in a hospital. For those with significant reading problems, the OSHA (Occupational, Safety and Health Administration) manual even allows for and encourages the use of symbols instead of words. This group represents the highest percentage of former dropouts who, under the elephant's plan, will be *"drop ins"*

No, the industry-search kids and those with severe reading problems won't be nuclear scientists, but they will learn the habits of work — self-discipline, a sense of building and belonging. And they will be needed in our workforce, at least until the left-brain robots take over. When that happens, we may all be in trouble!

Now let's return to the formula I presented at the beginning of the chapter:
If $SC \geq 50\%$
Then $NSC = (BC + HT + MA) - (AC + AA) = CCAS$

Where:

SC = selective creaming of 50% of students
NSC = neighborhood school captives
BC = blended classrooms
HT = high stakes testing
MA = midlevel academics
AC = advanced career studies
AA = advanced academic studies
CCAS = Causes of the crisis in American schools

two

The Solution: The Elephant-in-the-Classroom Plan.

Is there some way we can eliminate the killing fields and help our young friends, Emily and Jaylen? Our political representatives and school districts are charged with solving today's crisis in America, but the elephant respectfully requests that we look at her plan as one possibility. Our elephant is the problem, but she also gives us the solution.

Under the Elephant-in-the-Classroom system, we would still have a single blended classroom through the fifth grade, but an option for career studies would be available starting in the sixth grade. And in the ninth grade two paths would be offered: Full-time career or full time college prep. After the eighth grade, blended, uniform classes would not be taught. Students would be in advanced academic studies (AAS) or advanced career studies (ACS).

How it would work.
- In the second through the eighth grades, *all* students would be exposed to sample career vocations as well as basic academics. Let's call this a blended learning environment. Visitors to the classroom would discuss their successful business, craft, or service. The main push is exposure to career possibilities because students and their parents are already under the impression that college is the inexorable and natural outcome of school, the magical experience that guarantees achievement and financial success.

- Parents and students need to be shown the benefits of exciting non-college careers including, among other things, substantial earning power. The earnings of non-college entrepreneurs and other workers are impressive. (Independent electrical contractors, for example, may make twice the income of the child's classroom teacher). It may seem unfair that college-educated teachers make less than some "blue collar" workers, but we are living in a free market economic system based on supply and demand.

- In the sixth, seventh, and eighth grades, some parents and their children might opt for full-time ACS (advanced career studies) instead of remaining in a blended classroom. The reason students are given the opportunity to opt for full-time ACS at this age is to prevent burnout and drop out. Some students just can't wait until the ninth grade, when the two options are offered, to enjoy the benefits of ACS. If students choose ACS in the sixth, seventh, or eighth grades, they would not participate in comprehensive academic studies and therefore would not participate in annual state or federal achievement testing.

This initial career training is the type that would also develop academic skills needed for career certifications. One example is a digital tool such as Adobe Illustrator, which is a companion product of Adobe Photoshop. Photoshop is geared toward digital photo manipulation, while Illustrator provides typesetting and logo-graphic areas of design. In Florida, some children as early as third grade are already showing competency with this type of career training.

- If children and their parents opt for full-time career courses, ACS, in the sixth, seventh, and eighth grades, most of their time would be spent in career education. None of these students would be held back in middle school and none would take state or federal achievement tests. If our friend Emily could have enrolled in ACS in eighth grade, she could have avoided much subsequent pain and hardship.

Why not a preponderance of regular academic studies for most students after the eighth grade? *Because these are the killing fields.* This is where casualties pile up. These are the soldiers with no shoes clambering up Cemetery Ridge at Gettysburg in the face of murderous gunfire. This is where the teachers are pretending to teach college work and most students are pretending to study college work — until they give up or drop out.

The primary thrust of this book is to get students out of the killing fields and into relevant, productive, career education. The present system is clearly discriminatory because the majority of America's students are denied an education that teaches the skills and employment opportunities they need. It is a system of economic inequality. The elephant's plan will help close the employment gap, especially for poor children.

- **No blended classrooms**. In the ninth through twelfth grades, students would be in either ACS or advanced academic studies (AAS.) Blended classrooms would no longer exist.

- ACS students would spend most of their time in career training. In addition, they would have coursework in the reading and math necessary for their career training. Other learning might include courses such as U.S. History, citizenship, entrepreneurship, P.E. art, music, etc. Even though some of the career work is rigorous and qualifies for academic credit and even college credit, *my own preference is not to require full-time ACS students in the sixth through twelfth grades to take standard achievement tests administered by the state or federal government.* Oh, my God, did I say that? Yes, I did.

- AAS studies are for students who want to pursue a four-year university program and who have the academic ability, motivation, self-control, and ability to focus needed to succeed at that level. Students are eligible for AAS beginning in the ninth grade if they have earned above-average grades in sixth, seventh, and eighth grade classes, AND scores on an approved, norm-referenced national or state academic *achievement test* (not an IQ test) placing them in the top 30% compared to other students who are also completing the eighth grade statewide or nationwide (not as compared to students in their own school, who could be above or below average as a group). Students in the school lunch program would need to reach the top 40%.

Please note that the achievement test or tests would not be the state-mandated tests, which compare the student with benchmarks set up by the State Department of Education. Rather, an achievement test with national norms would be used.

The most common tests of this type are the *Stanford Achievement Test, 10th Edition* and the *Iowa Test of Basic Skills*. These are the types of tests required of private school students who participate in State Department of Education parental choice scholarship programs, such as vouchers. Section 1002.395(8) ©2, Florida Statutes. In addition, an interest inventory, such as *Ideas* can be helpful. Tests such as the *Stanford Achievement Test* and the *Iowa* are given annually in many schools today.

AAS students would need to maintain acceptable motivation and effort along with average or above grades in order to continue in the program. Students and parents would sign a contract that outlines proper motivation and behavior.

Students in AAS would continue advanced academic courses over four years (ninth through twelfth grades), working at a fast pace, with exposure to advanced placement classes and pre-Cambridge and International Baccalaureate type programs. They would take state mandated or federal achievement tests annually. AAS students could opt to transfer to ACS at the beginning of each school year.

- Students who are eligible for the free or reduced lunch program would participate in preschool programs such as Head Start and receive individual tutoring through the fourth grade, if they demonstrate weaknesses in reading and/or mathematics. (Children from families with incomes at or below 130% of the poverty level are eligible for free meals. Those with incomes between 130% and 185% of the poverty level are eligible for reduced price meals.)

- Children with learning disabilities or other problems would continue to obtain special help in the public school classroom, academic or career, through special classes, tutors, or private schools.

- The same would be true for children with special needs. Beginning in the sixth grade, special needs students could benefit greatly from ACS, learning skills leading to eventual community independence. While ACS would work with students of all ability levels, ACS programs would enhance the skills and self-esteem of special needs students. Many years ago, I had the privilege of consulting with a private association for intellectually-challenged students and we were able to set up a workshop where they produced beautiful and functional items. These products were sold to the public and resulted in a profit for the workshop.

- ACS students will receive evaluations from their teachers and instructors and organize portfolios demonstrating their competency on nationally recognized procedures. They could be given tests in design-related subjects and tests of basic skills such as reading and math. But these are locally developed, within-school tests, (not state-mandated achievement testing). They would help teachers and business representatives design effective career programs.

The portfolio is an important concept, especially for students in ACS. It would contain a record of career training along with completed projects, certificates, and industry-wide certifications. It would include awards, special interests, and accomplishments at home and in the community. Examples might include participation in team sports, dance, art, music, or volunteering. It would function as a job resume to help employers get to know the student's vocational accomplishments and life skills, as well as their character and personality. Thanks to Dr. Jon Reynolds, and Betsy Reynolds M.A., for emphasizing this concept for students in career studies.

Not all of these career courses would involve hands-on, mechanical work. Offerings could include customer service, leadership, marketing, computer support, robotics, restaurant-service, culinary arts, practical nursing, etc. But all programs would include the basic reading and math skills important for their specific vocations. (Please go to Appendix 2 for more offerings).

Career modules would reflect community needs and job openings. Many kids, such as Emily, have an interest in becoming a veterinarian assistant, for example.

- **No tests for ACS students.**
  Why no room for state or federal government tests which are presently used to compare schools and teachers? At least half of all students will be in ACS, and even though some students will have career-related academic work that could generalize to state or federal achievement exams, their ability to obtain certifications is primarily performance-based, not test-based. Most of their time and effort would be invested in career work, not academic work. Schools and teachers could be evaluated based on the number and quality of completed projects.

Of course, the Advanced Academic Studies group (AAS) would take state and federal exams each year or as often as necessary, but there would be no need to teach to the test. With this academic group, local, national, and even international testing may help in gauging the students' overall progress. These students would do very well indeed. So much for worrying about comparisons with Norway and China! If state tests show they are not achieving at a top-notch level, school administrators will want to know why. AAS is the program that our friend Jaylen needed to encourage him to work to his potential.

- At the end of each school year, students in ACS could opt to switch over to AAS, if they have the ability, self-control, concentration, and personal motivation. If they don't have these sturdy elephants' legs, they would have great difficulty keeping up with this more well-defined group of higher academic achievers.

I believe a majority of kids would prefer career studies because they are relevant and lead to something useful. Abstract academics can be boring and frustrating unless the student truly falls in the top range of academic intelligence and is interested in academic subjects. Students in ACS will have increased self-esteem because of competency and success.

We will need to increase and expand career modules and add instructors in order to provide more offerings and make them available at younger ages. But the primary change centers around attitudes, state laws, and school board directives — not a new structure.

A less well articulated approach is to simply add more career programs to neighborhood schools for students who haven't been creamed off to other selective schools and give these students an earlier exposure to career programs. This would necessitate changing district-wide testing requirements for career students, because they would be evaluated by their work product rather than state and federal tests. In this way, we could think of the base school building and all other places where students have been sent, based on selective factors, as one school.

Or, a new or revamped school building could pull all these programs together into one setting which would include within-school academic magnets, fundamental programs, and the stepped-up career programs. Fortunately, we already have many of the required ingredients. We need to challenge the college-for-everyone myth and start an early and serious move into career education, unencumbered by college-only academic testing, which would be replaced by hands-on success in career modules.

- **Free lunch.**
  Some children from poor families or from lower socio-economic backgrounds have more difficulty with academics in general, but could have the potential for college-prep courses at some point. This

is why, as a matter of fairness, students eligible for free or reduced lunch programs would receive preschool education and tutoring from kindergarten through the fourth grade, along with regular classroom work through the eighth grade.

- In addition, these students could be eligible for AAS studies beginning in the ninth grade if they have average grades in the eighth grade and achievement test scores placing them in the top 40% against state or national norms. If they don't meet that standard, but demonstrate a trajectory of progress in academic achievement that would put them into the top 40% by the end of the ninth grade, they would be eligible for the AAS program.

- In the eighth grade, a one-time achievement test would be used to determine eligibility for AAS, (or the average of two approved tests) based on national norms. This would not be the test mandated by the state and/or federal government which is currently used to compare teachers and schools. In many states, the present mandated state test would not help anyway, because it does not compare the student to state or national norms but rather to educational objectives established by each school system.

- Students not ready for AAS could still take a majority of college prep courses online from home. If they maintain above-average grades on these college prep level courses (or C average scores for kids in the free lunch program) for one year, they could automatically transfer to AAS. They could also take as many of the enhanced pre-Cambridge courses as they wish.

What about parents who insist that their child attend AAS, despite well-established difficulties with motivation, achievement, self-control, or the ability to focus? If the school administration and/or school board permits such a child to attend AAS, that child will be lost academically and have failing grades within one semester. He or she would also interfere with the progress of other AAS students. Meanwhile, many of that student's friends would be extolling the positives of ACS, reporting on their pride in creating and working on relevant and interesting projects.

- At this time, children with diagnosed learning disabilities are given full, individual IQ test batteries as a part of their diagnostic workup, and if they fall in the top 30% (or 40% if on the free lunch program) they could enroll in AAS.

- How about credits for high school graduation? Today, taking Florida as an example, a standard high school diploma requires 24 credits and a minimal grade point average (GPA) of 2.0 on a 4.0 scale. In the Elephant-in-the-Classroom program, ACS students would be offered two credits in reading, one credit in American history, one credit in citizenship, one credit in oral communications, one credit in entrepreneurship, and two credits in physical education. The balance of 16 credits would come from career modules. Academic studies needed to complete industry-wide certifications could include reading, math, or science instruction, *but only when needed to accomplish training in a specific vocational area.*

Some of these certifications lead to local community college programs and degrees. Internships would be sponsored by public and public-charter schools operated by the county as well as private industry, and could include work-study programs along with online courses and technical seminars. (Please go to Appendix 2 for examples of courses offering nationally accredited certifications).

- When ACS students complete the career modules they would graduate with an *ACS High School Diploma*. This could be as early as age 16 or as late as age 19, depending on rate of progress.

Some well-meaning critics may oppose a specialization system no matter how much sense it makes. What they don't realize is that we already have a subtle, efficient, but destructive dual system. Will they look the other way and permit the killing fields to continue? A less effective program would allow all students to try AAS and quickly wash out as they face true college-prep standards. This would result in much frustration for most students, including our Emily, and tempt well-meaning teachers and parents who still believe that college is the only acceptable outcome, to lower standards so that all students could "succeed."

But what about someone from a poor family in a poor neighborhood? What about a potential Abe Lincoln? We need to keep working on preschool programs even though long-term results are discouraging to date. We need to develop new strategies and give these kids at risk a better chance to be successful in academic and/or career fields. School officials "will need to continue to commit themselves to shrinking the achievement gap between white and minority students — whatever that takes." Opinion, Times Editorial, *Tampa Bay Times*, December 29, 2013.

The *Tampa Bay Times* is correct in pointing out achievement differences between white and minority students, but it may surprise you to learn that *the achievement gap is not racial*. Rather, it is a gap between kids from poor families and kids from middle-class families. This is a well-established fact and is no longer controversial. Here is one study: Randy L. Hoover, "A Re-examination of Forces and Factors Affecting Ohio School District 0AT and OGT Performance." Department of Teacher Education, Beeghly College of Education, Youngstown State University. Aug 26, 2008.

We also know that it is quite difficult to move from a lower social class to middle and higher levels. It isn't just a matter of poverty and lack of education. There is also a culture that resists upward movement because of a lack of trust in the system. The only way to overcome this immobility is good, well-paying, and interesting jobs along with the pride and skills inherent in the workplace. It may take a two or three generations, but the Elephant-in-the Classroom program offers the most direct route to elevating persons to their true potential.

After pre-kindergarten, kindergarten, four years of tutoring, and a total of eight years of school, students should have a pretty good idea where their strengths and weaknesses lie. This is not through IQ testing but rather through their own experiences, along with reviewing grades, achievement testing, and their own unique portfolio of work products. Children who are on the free or reduced lunch program would have a lower hurdle for entrance into AAS, as reviewed earlier. Also, these children may take as many of the advanced pre-Cambridge courses or online college prep courses as they wish, whether or not they attend AAS.

School counselors and school psychologists would assist students and their parents in determining each step in the student's academic and/or career journey. Vocational testing and surveys may help to define general areas of interest (as opposed to IQ or achievement testing).

I had the opportunity to meet Ben Weider of Level 6 Marketing, LLC, at a Pinellas Education Foundation meeting in March, 2014. He introduced me to a new program called Future Plans. After reviewing an individual's skills, interests, and values, Future Plans finds the best fit for career studies and educational studies, but the alignment is based on the youngster's experience and *careers-in-demand,* not just any of thousands of potential careers. Alignment between career studies and careers-in-demand is vital for successful employment.

Yes, under the elephant's plan Emily might have become a veterinarian assistant, assuming there was a demand for that position in her local community, and Jaylen could have completed college in three to four years.

Is it possible that a child might not have sufficient achievement scores and/or might not be motivated for college while only a middle-school or high school student but demonstrate brain maturation later on and ultimately attend college? This could happen, but this is not typical. It's important to deal with *probability* and not possibility when thinking about school policies. If a youngster with delayed brain-maturation completed ACS, she would finish school with excellent job skills. When her academic interest and ability improved, she would have no difficulty taking community college courses and moving on to a university or taking distance learning courses.

Would she have lost valuable time? Not really. I believe her choice would have resulted in the same type of student that attended college after World War II on the G.I. Bill. Those veterans were described as the finest students to ever enroll in America's universities. She would probably make it through college in 3½ years rather than five or six years and would have had excellent career experiences not found in most colleges.

What's the rush, anyway? Many men and women spend two or three years in the military, and rather than impede their careers it seems to help them. Whether it is the structure provided, or learning how to get along, or brain maturation, doesn't matter, but there is no reason for this headlong rush into college. Mormons sit out of college to go on two year missions. (Here's a little self-disclosure: I graduated with a bachelor's degree in business and served two years in the Air Force in England prior to entering a training program in clinical psychology).

If students in ACS later become interested in attending an academic college on a full-time basis, they can take courses in special precollege programs organized by their community college.

Of course, students may apply to college whenever they wish. Each college determines its own admission standards, including age and educational background. Students who participate in ACS may be of special interest to universities because of their broad background and experience. Some may have developed innovative projects or inventions that demonstrate unique abilities and most would have the discipline and social skills that come with on-the-job training.

What about the tiny fraction of students who are unable to benefit from even minimal career programs? Most of these unfortunate kids would continue to receive help through special therapeutic schools. A tiny fraction might not be capable of functioning in school. They would need help from other community institutions or become deserving welfare recipients. But the overall decline in drop-outs would help us win the war on poverty and lead to happy and contributing citizens.

The Elephant's Plan.
This represents a profound and necessary change in emphasis and direction. Today, most of our unselected students, who remain in the killing fields, are not receiving advanced academic studies (AAS) or advanced career studies (ACS).

I believe my job is to point out some great American myths and a mighty big elephant in the room, not to demand others deal with the elephant the way I would. Once folks are more aware of the damage incurred with our present system, and how creaming and individual differences in personality and brain function throw a new light on learning, county school boards, state legislators, governors, and the federal government might come up with better ways to implement a just and effective policy.

Once they do, they'll be able to visit a public school and not be saddened and embarrassed when they come face-to-face with an Emily or a Jaylen.

three

The First Great Myth: All Children have the Same Academic Potential.

> "Well, that's the news from Lake Woebegone, where all the women are strong, all the men are good-looking, and all the children are above average." Garrison Keillor, *A Prairie Home Companion.*

Now that we have seen how our system operates on both a personal and statistical level, we need to look at the factors that contribute to our present situation. There is a massive and rather clumsy elephant plodding through our schools, offices, and homes, yet this pachyderm is seldom seen. We don't see her because of a great American myth. Yes, a myth perpetuated by good and caring people, including our elected representatives. What is this myth? It is simply this:

All Americans are equal in ability regardless of personality, motivation, intelligence, or genetic inheritance.

A Lovely Myth

This is a lovely myth, no doubt. And most of us would like to believe it is true. After all, our Declaration of Independence promises us equal opportunity and a shot at life, liberty and the pursuit of happiness. Our forefathers also taught us to respect all people, regardless of rank or social class.

We might not like to think that one person is superior to another person, although each of us faces that reality daily when we finally recognize our own strong and weak characteristics, including such things as intelligence, memory, popularity, and athletic prowess.

We begin to realize that we remember things better when we see them as opposed to when we hear them, or we're better at ping-pong than track, or our reading skills are above or below those of others.

Unfortunately, we have received scads of awards for "most capable," "most improved," "friendliest," or whatever, and have sometimes come away with a false sense of accomplishment. Once we give up this fiction, a belief our loving parents graced us with — that we are perfect — we are happier and more successful with work, friends, and life in general. Emily and Jaylen are a good example here. They became friends and respected each other, even while recognizing differences in goals and aptitudes.

The absurdity of the concept of universal equality is made clear in Kurt Vonnegut's short story, "From Harrison Bergeron." One example given in that story was that the average height of NBA (basketball) players was close to 6'7", while the average American male was 5'9". The solution to that unfair situation was to set up average height rules that would require each team to offset taller players with shorter players. It was called the "midget – monster rule." And if a movie star ordinarily made $20 million from a hit movie, she would be paid $130,000 which is nine times the salary of the second assistant key grip. Bret Stephens, "Kurt Vonnegut's State of the Union," *The Wall Street Journal*, January 28, 2014. Would college students who support equality at all costs be willing to give part of their A grades to students with D grades? The high performers would then receive Bs and the underperforming students would receive Cs.

When I was in college, there were textbooks and courses titled *Individual Differences*. They seem to have disappeared. Are we less tolerant of individual differences today than we were 40 years ago? Maybe the myth of sameness and equality wasn't so persistent back then.

The elephant has four legs, but an examination of academic intellectual ability is necessary because this leg is buried deep beneath a blanket of mythology. And this leg is causing our elephant to bust up a lot of furniture. What is the name of this pivotal leg? Mental ability or I.Q.

This factor isn't mentioned anymore. Have you noticed? We don't see it for the same reason the elephant is ignored. *It scares us*. But it should have a significant and profound effect on education and public policy.

Oh no, you might be thinking. Not another psychologist who wants to segregate our students according to intelligence and discriminate against those who can't perform in the average or above I.Q. range, especially those coming from impoverished backgrounds.

Another "test 'em and reject 'em" philosophy, or even worse, a philosophy that searches for the "superman" and rejects the poor and un-washed that immigrated to our country and made it a "shining beacon on the hill."

Not to worry. No, the research doesn't lead us that way. In fact, I think that not seeing the elephant in the room is hurting low academic achievers more than high academic achievers. This results in dropouts.

Dropout.
How would you like to be labeled a dropout? Dropout of what? Out of the world, out of life, out of society? Out of the love and respect of your family and community? If I'm a dropout, then I guess everyone else is a *drop in*. Everyone else is great; everyone else is doing what they should be doing. I guess I don't have it. I have no future and need to live with my shame. Maybe a street gang will accept me — or show me how to make a few fast bucks.

Language is important. Words are important. Dropout doesn't sound good to me. But I guess we'll just keep referring to kids as dropouts when they're excluded from the best we have and confined to the holding cells of our impersonal, psychometric school system.

Yes, a big house of exclusion where we can ignore kids who don't fit, kids who don't try, and kids who are not academically brilliant. Maybe that'll teach them a lesson. Then we won't have to worry about them. "Thank God they're out of polite society and out of our hair." And the nice thing is that we don't have to feel guilty about their failure. We gave them every chance. Of course we did. And they blew it.

This book isn't about language, however. My goal is to convert dropouts into drop-ins and help the academic strivers as well as their fellow students who "fall through the cracks." The myth that perpetuates the elephant in the room means that we can't take an honest look at individual differences such as academic ability, gender, motivation, and a multitude of other traits and characteristics. In this case, the case of education, it's time to take a close look and see what we can learn.

I.Q. Made Simple

Let's examine intellectual ability. Merely acknowledging its presence will pay rich dividends for both Emily and Jaylen, and lead us out of the torturous labyrinth of American educational policies.

The concept of I.Q. is old-fashioned, all right, but we do need it. IQ testing originated with the work of Alfred Binet in France. He asked teachers to evaluate their students and was able to measure children's abilities by age level. His resulting assessment device was further developed by psychologist Lewis Turman at Stanford University and released in 1916 as the Stanford-Binet Intelligence Scale.

Even though I.Q. test construction has changed, please remember that the first investigation into mental ability was based on teacher observations of Western European children *in a school setting*.

Today, the Wechsler Intelligence Scale is the most widely used IQ test of those tests administered individually. The Wechsler is made up of subtests that purport to assess abstract verbal and spatial reasoning. Today, we also add subtests measuring short-term (working) memory and processing speed. It is not an achievement test. It does not measure reading, math, or spelling. Neither is it a vocational test designed to discover people's career interests.

The original concept of IQ is quite simple: If Jaylen, at age 10, does as well as an average 12-year-old on this lengthy battery of tests of broad abilities, he is given an IQ of 120 (12 divided by 10). That IQ places him at the 91st percentile, or higher than 91 out of every 100, 10-year-old children his age in the general population. Only nine out of every 100 children place higher than he does in general intelligence, as measured by this extensive battery of tests.

If Emily, at age 10, does as well as an average nine-year-old on this test, she is given an IQ of 90 (9 divided by ten). That IQ places her at the 25th percentile. So Emily does better than 25 youngsters her age and not as well as 75 youngsters her age. If these ability levels persist, and they usually do, Jaylen may have the intellectual firepower to attend an academic college, whereas Emily may have difficulty completing an academically-based high school.

I have to sidetrack here for a moment. When I first arrived in what was to be my hometown, I gave a talk about intelligence and mentioned that the Stanford-Binet could be used to assess basic intelligence at the age of 2 or 3. A local school supervisor stood up and suggested that my statements were not accurate.

"How can you test a child at that age," he barked. "He's not yet able to read!" (Let me again remind you, the reader, that individually administered tests of mental ability do not require reading and at that age should be used only to show that someone considered to be delayed actually has solid potential; not to put a ceiling on the child's potential).

The first time I gave the Wechsler Intelligence Scale in the "real world" — when it wasn't a supervised practice session — was to a 10-year-old boy in a rural school in Escambia County, Florida. The school had no testing office and there were no school psychologists in those days. And believe it or not, in at least one case I know of, the title School Counselor was assigned to the teacher who showed up last at the first staff meeting of the year! I administered the battery of tests on a card table on the stage of the school auditorium. This youngster wore no shoes. Whether he owned a pair, I don't know, but he told me he never wore shoes to school.

We can be biased about people based on appearance or background, and I thought this boy might have some difficulties with the Wechsler, but his responses to this highly reliable and valid test battery gave me a pleasant surprise. He scored with an IQ 110, which placed him at 75th percentile, or better than 75 out of 100 children his age. It's possible that he could have done somewhat better, because test conditions were not ideal, but the test helped to identify him as someone with good academic potential.

Since that time, I've become more suspect of intelligence test administration because I fear that some people who give them are not qualified or are breaking the strict rules of professional administration. Clinical psychologists are highly trained scientist – practitioners and the science part helps them understand the necessity for precise administration.

Because of their training, and because they administer these tests frequently, school psychologists, who work for the school system, are also expert in the administration of individual IQ tests.

But other test administrators may not be sufficiently trained. I attended a conference for teachers who were learning to administer the Wechsler Intelligence Scale for Children. The lecturer told the teachers how he achieved the highest test scores possible. He placed the child in a sound-proof room and dispensed M&M candy to keep the child focused and encouraged at all times.

The teachers thought this was wonderful. Another opportunity to help raise up a child (oh, you have to love the teacher's heart)! They didn't realize that artificially boosting a child's IQ score could put the child under great pressure and thrust her into situations she couldn't handle. In my opinion, teachers are not usually good test administrators, and test administrators are not usually good teachers.

In addition, proper administration of this battery of tests is costly and requires several hours for preparation, administration, scoring, and interpretation. Obviously, this makes it impractical for wholesale administration. And *group* administered IQ tests have limited reliability and validity. That's because they rely on reading comprehension and are administered in a group by a teacher, not a psychologist.

If I am complaining about IQ test administration, why do I think we need to value the concept of IQ? The answer is that over the years IQ has been validated for measuring a type of intelligence that is suited for advanced academic studies and various occupations. For example, most psychologists long ago established **an IQ of 110 or the 75th percentile as the minimal level for college attendance. If they were right, it means that only 25% (let's make it 30% to be on the safe side**) of high school students should go on to rigorous university work (although "dumbing down" has occurred in some colleges). That's another reason to use a generous 30th percentile and not the 25th percentile as a cut off point for college work.

I.Q. and Formal Education

130

120

COLLEGE
▲ TOP 25%
--------------------   110   --------------------

HIGH SCHOOL
▲
--------------------   100   --------------------

15% HIGH
SCHOOL

--------------------   90   --------------------
▼ BOTTOM 25%
NOT HIGH SCHOOL

80

60

This graph shows us that an abstract verbal IQ of 110 and above is expected for university work. But in addition to ability, the student will need the other three legs of the elephant which include motivation, ability to concentrate, and self-control. An IQ of 100 to 110 is needed for high school but 15% or so of the students falling in the 90 to 100 range can also graduate from high school, if they are motivated and able to concentrate.

Based on this analysis, I would expect that approximately 65% of students are capable of graduating from high school in four years. Some 35% of students would not be expected to complete a moderately rigorous academic high school.

Actually, the mean IQ of college graduates is not 110, but rather 115. The average college graduate places not at the 75th percentile but at the 84th percentile. Alan S. Kaufman, *Assessing Adolescent and Adult Intelligence*, Alan and Bacon, 1990.

Charles Murray reviewed the College Board's definition of college readiness and placed it at a 65% probability of getting a 2.7 freshmen grade point average or better. By that definition, only 10% of all 18-year-olds reach that level on the SAT. Charles Murray, "Do You Have Any Idea What an IQ of 110 is like?" Charles Murray, Cato – unbound.org.

All of this means that the bottom 45% may not succeed in a regular academic *high school*, either. The ACT college entrance exam confirms the IQ data because it suggests that 25% of high school graduates are ready for college. Also, advanced placement classes in high school are limited to a small percentage of high school students — and that is as it should be!

But intellectual ability of the academic IQ type is only *necessary; not sufficient,* to enable one to attend a legitimate college or university. In other words, it takes more than intelligence to belong in college.

Necessary but not enough.
Necessary, because the university should tap the top 25% and that means students falling at an IQ of 110 or above. Someone with a lower ability level

might struggle through a less competitive college in five or six years but this would mean giving up sports, socialization, and family time. It could add significant stress and lead to depression as well as increased financial debt. These things have to be talked about, and we need to be more aware of the abilities necessary for college.

Having an ability level in the top 25% doesn't guarantee college placement or success in college. The student may not work up to that ability level because of other difficulties, such as poor self-control, an inability to focus, or lack of motivation.

Highly competitive universities take the top 5% of graduates. This is based on scholastic aptitude tests and grade-point average. Less competitive universities take the top 15%. Other noncompetitive schools take the top 50%, or most students who apply, but should taxpayers support these institutions? Retaining the title "college," while lowering the academic standards to a high school level, is not the answer — but that's what we do. How about changing the name of the local police department to the Pentagon or changing the name of the local kite club to NASA. In Florida, community colleges are now called state colleges, and offer four-year degrees, but they have a strong focus on practical, two-year degrees, and career studies — thank goodness..

If parents want to pay their children's attendance at noncompetitive private schools, however, that is their prerogative. If these schools are well-run, they can serve as a valuable, abet, expensive bridge between adolescence and adulthood.

Hmm. *Maybe IQ as a predictor of academic success over the last century helps us to better understand our problems.* Our country has invested billions — make that trillions — to improve our schools so that all children can go to college. This is a well-meaning effort, and some good may have come from it, but it has created significant problems for both the academically inspired, such as Jaylen, and those who do not have the interest or the abstract-verbal or spatial-reasoning required for college, such as Emily.

What can we do about the IQ numbers? Is IQ hereditary? Can we improve it?

Heredity or Environment?

Okay. So this whole IQ business makes us all a little nervous, and it probably should. Let's take a closer look at intelligence and see if it helps to clarify things. First, does IQ result from heredity or environment? Please remember, when we speak of IQ we are simply talking about a person's mental age divided by their chronological age. So how does a child get a high or low mental age?

We know that heredity is important when we look at extreme cases such as a Mozart or Einstein and compare them with a mentally-challenged person. Mozart's brilliance showed itself so early in his life that it's difficult to believe it was the result of his environment. Yes, his father was an outstanding musician and tutored Wolfgang and his sister, but his sister showed none of the brilliance Wolfgang exhibited.

The same can be said of chess champion, Bobby Fischer. He started playing chess at the age of six, and nine years later became the U.S. chess champion. His explanation? "All of a sudden I got good."

While we are speaking of Einstein, I am reminded of a nice little story, perhaps a mythical one. Apparently, Einstein helped a neighboring elementary student with her math homework and she in turn helped him with his spelling. This could have happened, because at that time Einstein was a recent immigrant from Europe. This anecdotal story is also a reminder that achievement and IQ are quite different.

"Brain power is humanity's most important asset. It's one asset that never dies." This quote is from Aadith Moorthy, a 16-year-old student at Palm Harbor High School in Palm Harbor, Florida, one of 11 students in the world to receive a perfect score on the AP calculus BC exam. Lisa Gartner, "Academic Ace," *Tampa Bay Times,* December 3, 2013.

This does not mean that environment does not make a contribution to mental ability. Children with a less rich home environment may lack proper nutrition and may exhibit less confidence. They can also be easily distracted or marginally motivated in responding to test questions and school assignments. Studies show that these children often don't read as well as upper-middle-class children but, as with the youngster I tested many years ago in Escambia County, Florida, may still have good intellectual potential.

We see stories in the newspaper every day about people who have low ability levels. A college football player at a southeastern university was accused of stealing a motorcycle and a pair of shoes. He told police he found the motorcycle on the street — then wore the stolen shoes to the trial. A disingenuous California psychologist told upper-middle-class partygoers back in the '50s to pet a rock, claiming that the rock had feelings and would make a good pet. Some people believed him

In order to have a humane and competitive society, we need to ensure that those with fewer academic or career abilities, or those who come from disadvantaged backgrounds, have a safety net, as well as the opportunity to move upward.

Educational attainment in academic centers such as universities is accurately predicted by tests of mental ability. The average IQ of Americans with a high school diploma is about 99, and that score puts them above half of all persons their age and below half of all persons their age (middle average), while the mean IQ of Whites with a professional degree is about 125 or the 95th percentile. Most of the kids who go on to become professionals come from the upper-middle-class and may have advantages in terms of genetic predisposition, nutrition, and overall environment. Charles Murray, "Five Myths About White People, *Tampa Bay Times*, February 19, 2012.

Please remember that IQ tests are valid measures of abstract verbal and spatial reasoning. That's why they're such good predictors of college performance. But some children who do not perform at high levels on standard IQ tests may be more creative, more entrepreneurial, or have a higher potential for business and technical careers.

Several groups have challenged the stability of intellectual ability over time, or believe IQ can be changed. Malcolm Gladwell popularized the 10 year or 10,000 hour rule. He believes you don't have to be a genius to succeed; you just have to spend 10 years working at something for 20 hours each week. This is based on work by K. Anders Ericsson. "Is Genius a Simple Matter of Hard Work?" Terry Teachout, *The Wall Street Journal,* November 12, 2000.

Research has challenged the "10,000 hours of practice as a key to success," however. Scientists measured the working memory capacity of pianists and found memory made quite a difference. Pianists with above average working memory accomplished more in the same amount of time than pianists with less working memory. That being the case, the total number of practice hours required to achieve is much less for people with higher intelligence.

There may have been an increase in some IQ subtest scores over decades but no uniform increase in intelligence. James R. Flynn has examined cognitive trends over time and finds that individuals are stronger in some cognitive areas than in the past. Flynn suggests that people have greater abstract ability and that this ability is influenced by experience and culture.

But if we are really smarter today, we would expect to see an increase in all IQ subtests. This is not the case. Flynn's research is interesting and important, but it's not relevant to this book, because here we are comparing today's children with each other and not with children from previous generations. James R. Flynn, *What Is Intelligence?* Cambridge University Press, 2007.

Horse power.
Others have expressed the opinion that when someone reaches an IQ in the 120 range, additional IQ points don't translate into better production in the real world. But a subsequent study showed that participants who were in the 99.1 percentile of intellectual ability at age 12 were much less likely to go on to obtain a doctorate, secure a patent, or publish an article in a scientific journal than those participants reaching the 99.9 percentile. David

Hambrick and Elizabeth Meinz, "Sorry Strivers, Talent Matters," *The New York Times*, November 20, 2011.

Hambrick and Meinz go on to say "it would be nice if intellectual ability and the capacities that underlie it were important for success only up to a point. In fact, it would be nice if they weren't important at all, because research shows that those factors are highly stable across an individual's lifespan. But wishing doesn't make it so."

It is also clear, however, that being a genius is not necessary to succeed. If a genius level IQ were necessary, only 1/10 of 1% of the population would succeed at work. And nobody doubts that practice makes perfect, but practicing the wrong thing over and over, or at a very slow rate, doesn't help a person get ahead. The same is true if that activity is not important to the requirements of a specific job.

Boost your IQ.
A study in Hamburg, Germany subjected 20 young adults to one month of intensive training in juggling. They found an increase in the corresponding gray matter of the brain as early as seven days after training.

This is interesting, and we know that the brain can change (plasticity) and adapt to some degree to the environment, but there is no evidence that the broad, abstract abilities measured by IQ test batteries can be altered through repetitious activities. Intensive practice can raise test *scores* (not necessarily mental ability itself) but even those gains tend to subside after training. Sue Shellenberger, "Ways to Inflate Your IQ, *The Wall Street Journal*, November 29, 2001.

Because there is evidence of brain plasticity, writers continue to claim that broad changes in intellectual ability are possible through certain exercises. This is just not the case and it is unlikely that future studies will show anything different. Robert Lee Holtz, "As Brain Changes, So Can IQ," *The Wall Street Journal*, October 20, 2011

Video games.
Can video games increase IQ? Some studies have showed that when people are trained to play fast-paced, unpredictable games they score higher on lab tests measuring skills such as spotting fast-moving targets, tracking multiple objects, and grasping visual information quickly. Participating in these games could help someone doing rote work on an assembly line, or working in an airport control tower, but an increase in these specific skill sets has little to do with general mental ability.

"Unfortunately, no solid evidence exists yet to prove that such training has an effect on general intelligence. Furthermore, it's highly debatable as to whether such hypothesized effects might transfer in a durable way to human performance in practical, real-world contexts outside the psychological laboratory." David E. Meyer, "Do Mind Games Net Brain Gains" by Judith C Tingley, *Michigan Today*, January 30, 2014 ("Brain in the News," *The Dana Foundation*, March 2014).

Dr. Roy Baumeister's research at Florida State University leads him to believe electronic games help self-control, because of the constant monitoring built into the games and the perseverance required to do well. And self-control is one of the elephant's four sturdy legs needed for college work.

Neil DeGrasse Tyson, an astrophysicist at the Hayden Planetarium in New York, dislikes the word intelligence and believes people either want to learn, are ambivalent about learning, or reject learning. Evidence cited in this article shows that seventh graders, who were primed to think about the brain as not totally fixed but rather having potential for growth, were more *motivated* in math.

Motivation is important in learning, but just realizing the brain is plastic is not going to increase intellectual ability. Ken Bain, "Flummoxed By Failure — Or Focused?" *The Wall Street Journal*, July 14 – 15, 2012.

I think we all understand that achievement requires more than elbow grease. While persistence, hard work and high energy levels are important for success, *we need to emphasize jobs and activities we can comprehend*. Motivation is also influenced by the difficulty of work assigned. Kids who have trouble with abstract, verbal reasoning or who are required to work at too fast a rate are likely to become discouraged and give up.

Rate.
Rate of learning is important. More people could be physicians if they had 20 years to complete medical school rather than 10 years or less, but they don't have that luxury. At the same time, highly capable children become bored and discouraged when the work is too easy and they are not challenged.

Redefine IQ?
Well, if we can't change IQ, maybe we can call it something else or redefine it in a way that makes everyone happy! There has been much talk of multiple intelligences which break abilities into verbal intelligence, visual intelligence, music intelligence, touch and body-movement intelligence, mathematical and scientific intelligence, and social and self-insight intelligence. Thomas Armstrong, PhD, *Seven Kinds of Smart, Identifying and Developing Your Multiple Intelligences,* New American Library, 1999.

Trying to break intelligence down in this way tends to muddy the water, but it does force us look at other human capabilities and not put all our eggs in the basket of abstract, verbal abilities that are necessary for success in an academic high school or college. Students with these other special talents may be more successful than their academic peers if they are given the opportunity to develop these talents and abilities. As the elephant well knows, that's not happening as much as it should in our schools today.

Build a hammer.
When I was in high school, we were required to take a shop class. One of our assignments was to build a hammer. This required visual and kinesthetic skills, not to mention welding ability. It was frustrating work and my "completed" hammer reminded me of a sickly and impotent tomahawk. I was cruising toward an F, but a good friend built my hammer in the little time remaining, after he had finished his own hammer. I was happy and proud to pull a D grade! (Emily would have helped me too). I would estimate — and

this is pure speculation on my part — that as many as 60% of people with high-falutin' college degrees could not wire a lamp or prepare a gourmet dinner.

It is true that technical training that requires dexterity, imagination, and hard work often leads to a vocation, but so does an academic college degree. College students select a major because they are interested in a certain vocation, so let's try not to get too hung up on words such as technical or vocational.

If some of you think I'm denying the existence of high academic IQ functioning or hinting that it is not important — that is not my intent. There are individuals whose scores on IQ assessments place them in the top 1% or 2% of the general population, and who are capable of both academic work and right brain, hands-on spatial tasks.

In fact, psychologist Lewis Terman's original definition of the gifted child included only the top 1%, and these kids were taller, healthier, better developed physically, and superior in leadership and social adaptability. But at the 1% level, in a grade school with 200 children, there may be only two children that reach that level, depending on the makeup of the school.

Yes, Virginia, there really is such a thing as a super-bright person who can accomplish almost anything he or she sets out to do, if motivated and fortunate enough to have early childhood enrichment.

This does not include the author of this book, however, Virginia!

four

The Second Great Myth: All Kids are Pretty Much the Same

A chorus line.
We speak glibly about our students, as if they're all the same. Because of similar clothing styles, slouching to look cool, or letting their pants hang down in the back, they evoke a certain similarity. But they're all different. Remember the stage play, *A Chorus Line*? Yes, when you line them up they look the same, but when you ask them who they are, learn their history, and discover their strengths and weaknesses, you find they have much that is not in common.

So who the heck are they? This one's a right brainer and that one's a left brainer, this one seems tough but is emotionally tender underneath, this one's verbal and that one's nonverbal, this one pretends to care less, but is really motivated, while that one thinks school sucks. This one's clumsy and the guy with the huge shoulders is a jock, this one has trouble discriminating sounds and that one loves phonics. This one has beautiful handwriting (which she won't be using much anymore because of technology) and that one is so left-brained he writes like a physician — poor kid!

This one's an introvert and that one's an extrovert. This one's a daddy's boy, that one never had a daddy. This one gets to class early and that one's always late. This one smiles when he's angry and that one frowns when he's happy. This one's afraid of shooting his eye out with a BB gun and that one likes to steal hubcaps. This one can learn in one-to-one tutoring but can't learn in class, while that one can't learn unless she's in a group. This one cuts up in class because she's bright and bored and that one draws comic books in class because he's inspired.

Yes, all kinds, and that's what makes it interesting and fun. Some have a personality that is suited for college — and some don't. Future college kids such as Jaylen score high on the Educational Orientation Scale of the *Career Assessment Inventory*. Others, such as Emily, are low on that scale and high on the Mechanical Interest Profile. A test such as the 16PF (Adolescent Personality Questionnaire) developed by the Institute for Personality and Ability Testing, 2002, reveals other dimensions of personality. For example, some students score high on Concrete Thinking while others are high on Abstract Thinking. Some score high on Deliberate Thinking as opposed to Overactive and Easily Distractible.

Yep, not much in common. Yet we have a Common Core Curriculum because some good and earnest folks believe we need common benchmarks to better serve all students, even if there are significant differences between them. Students such as Emily need career assessments, not advanced academic benchmarks and high-stakes achievement tests, while students such as Jaylen may benefit from Common Core Benchmarks.

Can the elephant help us to understand and distinguish one student from another? Maybe so. *Proceedings of the National Academy of Sciences*, 2014, reveal that wild elephants can distinguish between human languages, and they can tell whether a voice comes from a man, a woman, a boy or a girl. Wow! So maybe we ought to let the elephants do it! *Just kidding, folks*, but I believe the Elephant-in-the-Classroom program will acknowledge disparities and try to give students what they want and need.

Elephants, horses, and "beatles."

Horses.
The current system reminds me of the differences between race horses and quarter horses. Race horses run for long distances, such as a mile and a half. They're a bit on the nerdy side and require lots of exotic training — and they

can be temperamental. They are an elegant and beautiful sideshow as far as other horses are concerned.

Quarter horses or ponies are extremely quick and specialize in short races, but they are also useful for recreational riding, rounding up cattle, and performing in rodeos. They are much more real-world than the racers and fun to ride. I once saw a race at the Hialeah Racetrack in Miami, Florida between the winner of the Kentucky Derby and a champion quarter horse. The quarter horse took off like a shot and left the race horse far behind. At about the half-mile mark, the racehorse took the lead and ended the race far ahead of the quarter horse. I wondered how the race horse would do in the real world of rough terrain, rounding up cattle.

What if we raise and train quarter horses in exactly the same way we raise and train race horses? Same exercise, same food, same practice. The race horses will be thoroughly frustrated because the quarter horse can't keep up in the long stretch but the quarter horses would be equally frustrated because the race horses lack versatility and can't keep up for short distances. I think there would be some angry exchanges and maybe a few nips on the horses' flanks. What a ridiculous idea you might think — but this is what we do in our school system today.

Both types of horses have different living styles and goals. Neither is better than the other and each would like to fulfill its destiny. The cowboy would never choose a racehorse for rounding up cattle and the Queen of England would feel silly sitting on a rambunctious quarter horse while wearing her supersized hat to the Ascot races. The cowboy needs a quick, responsive, and agile horse, while the Queen wants a beautiful, safe, and well-mannered mount.

This analogy also holds up from a financial point of view. Graduates with tech-field associate degrees (quarter horses) eclipse bachelor's degree holders (racehorses) after one year in the work force, but earnings from the four-year degree surpass those of the lesser degree five years after graduation. This gap grows to $7000 per year after 10 years. My own calculations indicate that it may take 20 years before the race horses pay off their higher costs and take the lead in the financial race with quarter horses. Mark Peters and Douglas Belkin, "Bachelor's-Degree Payoff Can Seem Elusive," *The Wall Street Journal*, June 25, 2014.

Beatles.
Here's another analogy: what if the Beatles musical group and the four operatic tenors had trained and performed together? I don't think the performers would have been happy and customers would have demanded their money back. Each did something different. The tenors were appreciated by a small segment of society and the Beatles were appreciated by a larger segment of society. Was one better than the other? No.

Writers' like to do things in three's, so here's another musical analogy. We will train musicians with the New York Philharmonic Orchestra in the same way we train Jazz and Blues musicians. Good idea? Sounds democratic and fair, but it's not going to work.

Are we presently hurting the quarter horses, the four tenors, the New York Philharmonic and the Beatles? Yes we are. But more importantly, we're hurting Emily and Jaylen.

Here's an example of how this mixed educational picture negatively affects the potential advanced academic student (AAS). Michael Petrelli, executive vice president of the Fordham Institute and a former U.S. Education Department official stated, "Let's be honest about the trade-offs. I seriously question the effectiveness of the campaign to get as many students as possible, even those with so-so academic records, into advanced placement courses."

According to Bill Maxwell, a writer for the *Tampa Bay Times*, school districts are scrapping programs such as after-school science labs designed for advanced placement classes. And advanced academic students are also losing out because many excellent teachers are released or transferred. Maxwell goes on to say, "I support efforts to help our lowest achievers, but like Petrelli and others, I believe we have tipped the scales and are ill serving our highest achievers." Bill Maxwell, "Achievers Lose Out," *St. Petersburg Times,* October 16, 2011.

When Maxwell says our highest achievers, I believe he's referring to our highest *academic* achievers. Many of our highest achievers are *career types* who are needed to build our economy — as any employer will tell you. But the mixed educational picture is hurting them as well. Our career types have little interest in abstract academic learning. They want to touch, feel, and smell their work — and let their creative juices flow.

Now we are dragging these right-brainers into the academic part of our brain, for which they have little use. These are the visual and kinesthetic learners, but they're required to stumble along in watered-down academic high school courses. This often leads to dropping out, boring, low paying employment, or worse yet, crime and welfare. Should Emily and Jaylen have attended the same classes in high school?

No.

Different students have different needs and when we examine all these factors and add them to abstract mental ability, middle-school achievement scores and grades, along with motivation and self-control, we will have a close approximation of which kids will benefit from career education and which kids will benefit from college-prep. Most of this will be student self-selection. If given the opportunity to choose, most students will know what makes sense to them.

Here's a quote from a student named Dakota Blazier: "I discovered a long time ago that I'm not book smart. I don't like sitting still, and learn better when the problem is practical." Tamar Jacoby, "This Way Up," *The Wall Street Journal,* July 19 – 20, 2014

College-bound kids enjoy and excel in traditional academic subjects while career-bound students enjoy and excel in career instruction. But all kids need the opportunity to show us which areas they're good at and which they prefer. And, of course, not all career-oriented kids or college-oriented kids are the same.

If college-oriented students were forced to give up their academic studies and take only career courses, many would resent it. But they've never been asked to do that. Yet career-oriented kids are often forced to take academic work and give up an opportunity for career courses! Courses they would love and excel at. Is that fair? Counselors may not refer them to these career programs because the students' schedules are too tight. And they're tight because the school is graded according to success on academic achievement scores. So if they don't do well, they retake the courses and tests umpteen times until they do, leaving no time for advanced career studies (ACS).

Students also waste valuable time taking extra remedial courses in order to pass the state achievement tests. These are the very kids who need career programs but can't get them because these career programs are requiring mandated scores on *academic* tests as a requirement for taking these primarily *non-academic* courses! Emily knows all about this. Talk about doing things backwards! Where is Alice (in Wonderland) when we need her? But the schools are required to follow state and federal guidelines so the child won't be "left behind" in their "race to the top" — top of what? A political fairy tale?

If you ask one of these career kids why they don't like the courses they sit through all day long, a day crammed with chemistry, social studies, and foreign languages (two years required), here's what you're likely to hear:

"Not relevant. Not relevant. Not relevant. Not relevant. Not relevant." But when she's talking to her peers she might say: "It sucks. It sucks. It sucks. It sucks. It sucks."

We know more about the brain than we did in the past. Instead of looking at the brain as we might have 100 years ago, we now feel more confident that we can differentiate different types of learners who utilize different areas of the brain. The more we "discriminate" in this way, the more happy and successful our students will be.

It's the students who are now pressured into the regular, blended academic program who are the real losers. Students with career preferences are not getting what they need and students with college preferences are not getting *enough* of what they need. Many students, especially the less academically motivated, are wasting their time until they drop out — or until they take GED (graduate equivalency courses) so that we can all pretend they are regular graduates of Lake Wobegone High School

This may surprise you, but there is increasing research evidence that the wide ranging, broad learning we encourage in high school and college may actually be in tension with focused expertise in a particular skill. If students are pressured into the regular academic high school curricula, they could lose some ability to perform in technical and creative areas, such as making a soufflé. These students may persist through the academic high school and receive a watered-down degree, but they may lose something important in the process. Alison Gopnik, "What's Wrong with the Teenage Mind?" *The Wall Street Journal*, January 28 – 29 2012.

What about left brain, right brain?
While both sides of the brain are necessary for any thought or activity, some people are more attuned to right-brain strategies while others rely on left-brain strategies

Our students have many neurological and personality differences. Right- brainers are more associated with hands-on, spatial thinking while left brainers are more associated with abstract verbal reasoning and the sequential curriculum used in most schools.

Academic intelligence and academic IQ are important and necessary, but some individuals are less linear in their thinking and given to spatial and creative learning.

In order to unmask the brain, it's important to look at the research on brain architecture, and this research begins with the idea of hemisphericity. Now there's a 50-cent word! The concept of hemisphericity is by no means new. Nineteenth century physicians speculated that the two hemispheres of the brain had an ingrained dislike for each other but had finally, grudgingly, learned to live together.

Spectacular findings.
In 1844, British physician Arthur Ladbroke Wigen contended that the two hemispheres possessed independent minds, and functioned in a coordinated fashion only because they had learned to do so. In 1981 Roger Sperry won the Nobel Prize for showing how the two hemispheres of the brain could communicate effectively with one another. Molfese and Segalowitz, 1988, state that "differences in thinking style may be relatable in some way to individual differences in hemispheric organization or characteristic patterns."

When news of these spectacular findings reached the general public, it opened a Pandora's Box of speculation and misinformation. Countless books were published, but the speculation outran the evidence and led to "dichotomaina," a belief that *all* thinking and behavior could be assigned exclusively to the left or right hemispheres of the brain, and that each hemisphere could operate separately from the other and separately from other areas of the brain.

Because of the exaggeration and speculation surrounding this area, I dismissed the findings and went on to other things. But then something interesting happened. I began to notice that some of my counseling clients revealed personality traits that mimicked the original findings supporting hemispheric differences in thinking and personality. In addition, the learning styles of many students in my schools were also consistent with this earlier research. That puzzled me. Did the researchers back off too soon, or was I seeing things that didn't exist? This dilemma motivated me to go back and review both the original investigations and current research.

What I found is that the original insights are still valid and intact. The early investigations into hemispheric differences provide us with rich new concepts and vocabularies to help us better understand the human personality. These concepts and behaviors are based on promising research rather than the subjective and anecdotal findings that support most personality theories.

Hemisphericity.

Now that we've cleared the air somewhat, let's discuss the core qualities or central tendencies of the theory of hemisphericity. *The core of the theory is that the personalities of some individuals are significantly influenced by the strategies of one hemisphere more than the other hemisphere, and that this personality structure can influence thoughts, emotions and behavior. Some individuals are affected only slightly by hemispheric personality factors and simply use hemispheric strategies that correspond to the task at hand. Knowledge of this hemisphericity (or hemispherality) can be useful in understanding and predicting behavior.*

But aren't the hemispheres more similar than they are different? In most individuals, the degree of superiority in the competence of one hemisphere (versus the other hemisphere) is probably not great. Is a genetic predisposition (modified by the environment) sufficient to create and sustain a specific hemispheric personality structure? One of the answers to this question is the "winner take all" principle: If right hemisphere strategies work "only" 20 percent better than left hemisphere strategies for five-year-old Travis, fear of failure might push Travis to use right hemisphere strategies *all* of the time.

For example, if Travis can learn to read by visualizing the shapes of the words (right brain) rather than using sequential, auditory, phonetic analysis (left brain) of letters, then he will do so. Because of this, Travis may become a terrible speller and may encounter some reading difficulties in later grades, but reading through visual pathways will be easier for now.

In math, he might solve abstract problems without using sequential, step-by-step rules for solving these problems. Because of his inability to verbalize the methods he uses, he may even be accused of cheating, but his reliance on right-brain strategies will grow stronger with time. And his right-brain superiority may push him toward social skills and sports at the expense of academics. The principle of "use it or lose it" also comes into play in regard to his less used left-brain strategies, which may lose some of their functional proficiency.

There are many other findings and theories related to learning, including studies of working memory and contrasts between higher and lower cortical areas (comparing brain preference vertically, up and down, versus the comparison of the left brain versus the right brain.). Neuropsychological research is touched on here in order to give the reader greater awareness of individual differences in students.

Learning strategies.

We all know people who use left-brain strategies to learn. These strategies tend to be sequential, literal and logical, and the individual shows more interest in facts and details than the creative process. These folks will be found in occupations such as engineer, bookkeeper and teacher. Right brainers, on the other hand, tend to be imaginative, spontaneous, and easily bored. Occupations include sales, art, and architecture. The left side of the brain, which emphasizes verbal and sequential thinking, is highly suited for an academic high school and college education, but right-brain skills are needed in career studies and vocational careers.

Other types.

Understanding left-brain and right-brain personality styles is an important factor in school reform, but there are many other types of abilities that influence learning. Most professionals do not refer to them as additional types of intelligence because we don't have the research or tests and measurements to establish the reliability and validity we find with IQ testing. But they are just as real and are powerful influences on behavior and learning.

When I previously discussed IQ, I mentioned Thomas Armstrong, PhD, who wrote a book called *Seven Kinds of Smart,* which refers to multiple intelligences. Checklists for determining individuals' strongest and weakest ways of being "smart" include verbal intelligence, which is the one measured so reliably by intelligence tests and which is so important for college work, but also include visual learners, the musically talented, those with strong body awareness and kinesthetic skills, logical smartness, and people-smart, which is identified with a strong social sense.

Also, about the same time, Daniel Goleman, PhD, wrote a best-selling book titled *Emotional Intelligence, Why it Can Matter More Than IQ*. His very readable book includes chapters on "Managing with the Heart" and "The Roots of Empathy." Armstrong, Goleman, and other writers have identified traits we are aware of, but rarely have room for in our stampede toward college and the state and federal testing that accompanies it.

Right-brain admissions.
Some college admissions offices are beginning to recognize that the emphasis on academic test scores, speaking ability, essays, and interview favors the left-brain student, and that they may be losing some of their most creative college applicants. Many creative individuals are bored by linear, sequential learning such as reading philosophy books and writing long academic papers.

A few educators believe the SAT and the ACT are not the best predictors of future academic performance. Some schools, such as Bard College in Annandale-on-Hudson, New York, are using a 2,500 word research essay to determine admissions. If the student receives a B+ or better grade on the essay, regardless of SAT or ACT scores or high school grades, they will be admitted to Bard.

This sounds nifty, but it's impractical and may encourage cheating. Who will keep track of who actually writes the essay? It will also put pressure on the college administrators to give higher grades on the test when more enrollments are needed — especially from wealthy applicants. Bill Maxwell, "Essays, as the New Test," *Tampa Bay Times*, October 6, 2013.

Some colleges are also beginning to assess an applicant's total body of work. If a student has invented a process or product that is viable or won awards at regional science fairs, this is important information regardless of the student's grades or achievement scores.

If high schools would like to adopt this strategy of reviewing a student's body of work, or requiring an essay in order to assign the student to AAS — in addition to achievement scores and grade average — that would be fine.

I am only presenting one possible way to implement this Elephant-in-the-Classroom program. Local school districts will develop their own strategies. My purpose is to encourage and support those efforts.

If the student's parents are the ones who actually develop the projects for presentation at science fairs, (remember, scholarships to some prestigious universities amount to $200,000 or more over four years) or someone at the school reveals the subject matter of the qualifying essay in advance, a child might get into AAS even though not qualified, but would face the prospect of a fast-moving college-prep program that will expect good grades in a competitive environment and high levels of motivation and effort.

Students who aren't best suited for advanced academic studies, or lack interest and motivation for that style of learning, can sign up for career studies. They will acquire usable skills and perhaps monetary rewards, and can still *loop back* through certification programs, two-year associate of arts or science certificates, a college bachelors degree and onward to Harvard and a Ph.D. if they have the ability and motivation to do so.

Our career students will have a better future in career studies than in the present school environment, where discipline problems and a smorgasbord of college prep, reading, and vocational studies lead to failure — leaving them confused and unprepared for the real world of work.

Again, ask Emily.

five

The Third Great Myth: All Kids should go to College.

The case against college.
Let's look at the case against college. The insistence that every child can and should attend college has created a bottleneck that hurts those who are qualified for college and an even greater barrier for those who are not qualified for abstract academics — kids who should be turning their many talents in other directions.

So why this love affair with college? Many Americans think college equals success and they naturally want the very best for their children. Similar to infatuation, this love affair may not last long.

Most children should not go to college.

Substantial numbers don't complete college in four years and are not successful financially. This misperception may go back to the White Anglo-Saxon Protestant (WASP) elite that ran our country in the 1800s. They have supposedly been replaced by a meritocratic system which is based on talent, but many still strive, consciously or subconsciously, for the Yale, Harvard, Princeton community, and the contacts that maintain the old establishment.

Bruce McCall, a successful writer who was a high school dropout, commented on his doubts about succeeding in New York City. "Everybody knew that everybody connected with the smart magazines came from old money; went to Harvard, or at least Yale, summered on the Cape, married a deb; recited Horace while playing squash; and mixed with literary royalty at chic dinner parties in Manhattan penthouses. From graduation day onward, this superior breed trod an endless red carpet to various forms of glory." Bruce McCall, "Confessions of a High School Dropout," *Town & Country Magazine,* August 2013.

Social snobbery.
The cultural critic, Camille Paglia, was quoted in *The Wall Street Journal* as saying that what's driving the push toward universal college graduation is "social snobbery on the part of a lot of upper-middle-class families who want the sticker in their car window." Bari Weiss, "A Feminist Defense of Masculine Virtues," *The Wall Street Journal*, December 28 – 29 2013. That's being a little harsh on parents who just want the best for their kids, but it is time to take a fresh look at these core prejudices.

According to Joseph Epstein, the merit in our meritocracy may not be genuine. "The only thing that normal undergraduate schooling prepares a person for is — more schooling. Having been a good student, in other words, means nothing more than that. One was good at school. One had the discipline to do what one was told, learned the skill of quick response to oral and written questions, figured out what professors wanted, and gave it to them." "The late, great American WASP," Joseph Epstein, The Wall Street Journal, December 21 – 22, 2013.

This perception of college as the preferred goal for all students is the most difficult single problem that must be overcome if we are to allow individuals to flow naturally toward their own inclinations and abilities.

Most parents, especially middle-class parents, have one question when visiting friends they haven't seen for a while. "How's Janie; where's she going to college?" Of course, it is assumed that she *is* going to college. If she isn't, the friends might see Janie's parents as failures and the parents themselves would feel embarrassed. Some high schools have debate teams that debate other schools, and sometimes this competition is advertised not as a debate between high schools but as a "college bowl." Other high schools in wealthy areas are given names such as "University High School."

If we accept the college-for-everyone concept, these reactions would be understandable, but there are two underlying assumptions to this position that are not valid. The first assumption is that student failure has to do with parents not pushing their kids hard enough, rather than students' ability level or motivation. The second assumption is that with concerted effort *all* students can be helped. Helped to do what? It's always a nice idea to give students extra help in anything, but fattening them up to satisfy the voracious appetite of state achievement tests? Maybe not. And maybe the failing students are trying to tell us something.

The only way to counteract this misperception is success in the real world of ACS graduates. This will take time because of built-in stereotypes and prejudices against these students. After all, left-brain academicians make up a large share of our country's cultural critics and writers. These folks believe they are the best and brightest — and even the happiest. This carries over to newspaper and television programming as well. But psychological research has consistently shown that after people acquire a solid but modest income, additional monies do not create sustained happiness.

In some ways the university world is a non-real world. It's a think tank, a finishing school, and a self-congratulatory system that feeds the ego. But it is also an incubator of professional classes such as professors, physicians, lawyers, accountants, engineers, and scientists. From this system, our country expects leadership and the discovery of things that presently don't exist. These innovations will come from the top 1%-10% of our academic strivers.

U-Rah-Rah!
Why do 90% of parents and students insist on an academic university — besides the success of the football team? *Perception, pure and simple.* The perception that a four-year university degree is essential to happiness and wealth and is the only door to a better life.

This is a great American myth, that an academic university degree always offers more opportunity than community colleges or technical fields of endeavor. Politicians at every level insist that all children should attend college, thus raising a false standard. Parents want their children to "make it" and this means attending the most prestigious university available.

Dr. Jon Reynolds, a former superintendent of schools, told me that the parental belief that college is for everyone is a myth and is extremely harmful to students and schools. Furthermore, after many years in public education, he believes the concept that all children are willing to learn academics is also a myth. Teachers may be sending good messages and trying to draw students out, he says, but this is not always possible because "some students have their receivers turned off."

Are we sending kids to college that shouldn't be there? The proportion of society's resources going to fund higher education has tripled over the past half-century but at least 40% of full-time students entering four-year programs fail to have a degree in six years. In most universities, the four-year graduation rate is less than 30%. "Do Too Many Young People go to College?" *The Wall Street Journal*, June 25, 2012.

Will power, self-control and the ability to focus.
And students seeking a college education need more than high IQ numbers. Roy Baumeister, PhD, social psychology professor emeritus at Florida State University is co-author with John Tierney of *Willpower: Rediscovering the Greatest Strength*. According to Baumeister and Tierney, will power and self-control are necessary for success. Types of self-control include intellectual, emotional, performance, and impulse control. They are necessary for advanced academic studies.

Children start learning self-control as early as infancy. Crying at night is one example. If parents do not rush to their crying child's side, but rather let the child cry for a fixed period and then offer comfort, followed by withdrawal for another fixed period, the infant begins to learn self-control and after repeated sessions will go to sleep without help.

It takes effort and a stable early environment to teach self-control. This is why children raised by single parents may not do as well in life. Kids from two-parent homes get better grades, are healthier, and have greater emotional stability. *Willpower, Rediscovering the Greatest Strength,* Penguin Press, 2011.

Self-control is partly hereditary, but also requires stability and monitoring. Again, students from upper-middle class families may have an advantage here. It is possible for someone to have a high IQ score, but less self-control, and I might add — less creativity. And some may have a lower IQ score, but possess tremendous willpower and self-control. Ronald Alsop "Gotta Have It Now," *Notre Dame Magazine,* Winter, 2011 – 12.

The truly elite.
Yes, there are some individuals who are not only academically bright, but have high aptitude for technical and creative thinking. These folks will do very well in the university setting and go on to become professors, lawyers, physicians, engineers, and research scientists. But the ACS folks will hold their own against many college graduates and, in fact, may create more wealth than college graduates, including the professions mentioned above. And they will also get there a lot sooner.

Some academically inclined students attend college to immerse themselves in the humanities. This is a good thing, but it's not for everyone. If we go back to psychologist Abraham Maslow's hierarchy of needs, surely getting a job comes before self-actualization.

Despite the enormous financial burdens imposed by college tuition and room and board, along with the fact that many students take six years to "complete" a four-year program and then have trouble finding a job, the idea persists that parents who have a student at a university have bragging rights. These bragging rights come from the reputations of institutions such as Duke, Stanford, Notre Dame, and many high-caliber state universities. These are the academic elitists. They are proud of themselves and their institutions, as well they should be.

Right-brain, practically-minded students can have bragging rights too, if we permit that to happen. A February, 2013 report by Jon Marcus of the Hechinger Institute (a service of CNN, Fortune, and Money) indicates that a graduate with an associate degree from a community college started work as a computer networking engineer at a local TV station making about $50,000 a year. That is 15% higher than the average starting salary for college graduates — not only from community colleges, but for bachelor's degree holders from four-year universities.

An interesting video developed by Kevin Fleming @Telosis.com, demonstrates the 1, 2, 7 formula, which Fleming claims is as true today as it was in 1950. For every job requiring a master's degree or above there will be two jobs requiring a bachelor's degree and seven jobs for those with career skills.

Fleming's research shows that the *average* earnings range for the associate of arts degree is $27,000 to $68,000 whereas a business manager with a bachelor's degree falls in the range of $34,000 to $97,000. But one must also take into account skills and abilities. The most accomplished individuals with an associate of arts degree can reach $86,000, while the bottom range of bachelors' degree manager is $56,000. And those choosing career education avoid at least $50,000 in lost wages and college debt.

I'm thinking that the elephant may be shaking her weary head again because the 25% to 30% of college graduates who can really benefit financially from that education, especially those majoring in finance, engineering, accounting, etc. are pulling up the overall average earnings for college graduates. These statistics utilize a *mean average* to compare university and career students, but they need to use a *modal average*, which would show the average income of most college graduates.

Why is a *mean average* not useful here? If I'm thinking of buying a house in a certain neighborhood with twenty-one homes and the realtor says the average home is worth $$643,000, I might be surprised to learn that most of the homes are valued at $75,000, except for the Russian oligarch whose home is worth $12 million — not counting his yacht. This *mean average* is calculated by adding the value of all homes and dividing by the number of units. The *modal average* is calculated by finding the most common home value. In this case, $75,000.

Based on this statistical analysis, the projected income of career graduates would be a lot higher than many college graduates, especially those majoring in the humanities and other non-career type college programs.

Here's another example of a technology background leading to financial success. Brian Chesky attended the Rhode Island School of Design where he majored in illustration and industrial design. He and a friend were low on money and wondering how to pay their rent, which was coming due. A design society convention was taking place in San Francisco and knowing that hotel rooms would be scarce, they used three air mattresses and turned the apartment into an "air bed and breakfast."

Now, a few years later, the 32-year-old co-founder of Airbnb has a business valued at $2.5 billion and 500,000 properties available in more than 190 countries. This is an extreme example, no doubt, but illustrates what an entrepreneur with technical training, and without a liberal arts college degree, can accomplish. Andy Kessler, "The Weekend Interview with Brian Chesky," *The Wall Street Journal*, January 18 – 19, 2014.

According to Jeffrey Corliss, a graduate of the Motorcycle Mechanics Institute, there will be more than 1.4 million job openings in the collision, automotive, diesel, motorcycle, and marine industries. Before attending the Motorcycle Mechanics Institute, Corliss received a bachelor's degree from Michigan State University. Jeffrey Corliss, "Trade Schools Deserve Seat At The Higher Education Table." *The Tampa Tribune*, May, 2014.

Josh Mandel reports that Pioneer Pipe, an Ohio firm, paid 60 of its welders more than $150,000. Two of its welders made over $200,000. The owner had to turn down orders because he couldn't find enough skilled welders!

Meanwhile, one-third of college-graduate bank tellers need public financial help. This statement by James Carville was found to be mostly true by Pundit Fact. "A Third of Tellers Need Public Help," Money, *Tampa Bay Times*, December 15, 2013.

A parent's dream.
Why would parents even consider giving up the dream of their child winning honors at a great university? My hope is that they will want what is best for their child. Emily's mother was praying for this possibility before Emily's hopes were dashed by government regulations. Parents will note that their child is not invigorated by academic learning and as a result does not have stellar grades. They might also see depression, anger, or a disruptive home environment because of the child's frustration and unhappiness in school. (Appendix 3 offers some guidelines for parents who are considering advanced career training for their child).

They will respect their child's special abilities and interests and realize that if their child wants to attend a university at some point, that option is still open. They won't want their child to experience failure or spend four years slogging through high school pretending to learn, and then be unprepared for a well-paying occupation in the real world. And how does one measure success, anyway? Making money? Being happy? Helping the community? Being part of a family or raising a family that contributes to society?

Parents might even think about their own future. The child who is unprepared to navigate the employment market will not have the kind of time or income necessary to assist his or her parents in their old age. Parents want happy, productive children who will care for them in their final years.

As Prof. Susan B. Neuman, assistant secretary for elementary and secondary education under President George W. Bush, stated, "obsessed with achievement score gains, policymakers seem to have forgotten that schools are designed to serve their local communities, to educate children deeply, not simply in basic reading and writing, but in the skills they have. We have undervalued knowledge in the information-based economy."

New approach.
There is a growing consensus for a new approach. The Pathways to Prosperity Project at the Harvard Graduate School of Education concludes that by focusing too

much on classroom-based academics, public schools shortchange large number of students who need preparation for careers not requiring a bachelor's degree. The authors are Ronald Ferguson and Robert B. Schwartz. They are recommending that beginning in middle school, students be provided solid preparation in real world career-oriented teaching and training that leads to appropriate college or certification programs. Bill Maxwell, "The Costs of College Obsession" *St. Petersburg Times*, February 20, 2011.

Careers not requiring a bachelor's degree? There is still the clear implication that with a bachelor's degree one can do it all, but some jobs just don't require all that "marvelous" learning. Take it from me, a bachelor's degree does not teach you a lot of things. I have a Ph.D. and can't make a hammer!

There are even rumblings in Massachusetts, a state that has led the nation in academic achievement. A business group has called for new opportunities to innovate through educational career offerings such as interactive social media lessons, adaptive learning and assessment platforms, digital gaming, and accelerated learning challenge grants. "Despite Lofty Goals, Massachusetts Advised to Set New Educational Goals," Sean Cavanaugh, *Education Week*, April 1, 2014.

A lengthy editorial in *The New York Times* endorsed more flexible curricula for American students *"with greater choice between applied skills and the more typical abstract courses!"* (Author emphasis). According to the *Times*, very few high schools offer career or technical education and any deviation from the classical education is viewed with suspicion. "Research has shown that the right mix of career and technical education can reduce dropout rates, and the courses offered don't have to be from the old industrial arts ghettos." Editorial, *The New York Times*, December 8, 2013.

Wishful thinking.
Is all of this just wishful thinking? Will Americans ever accept individual differences and oppose the requirement for academic instruction and testing for career-bound students? Never, you say. Too many people are benefiting from today's broken system, people who don't want to kill the golden goose. And politics, of course.

But what about feminism? How much have aspirations for women changed in only 30 years? What about gay-rights? Another cultural transformation that acknowledges individual differences.

Maybe we're just stuck in a cultural window. Maybe all this university hype is fairly recent. Sometimes we don't pay enough attention to history. We complain about the deadlock in congress and dirty politics employed by senators and congressional representatives today. We forget about the politically-motivated physical assaults that took place during the Civil War, when, for example, U.S. Representative Preston Brooks brutally beat Senator Charles Sumner with a walking cane.

We also forget that 19th century land-grant laws ushered in our state university system, a system emphasizing *career instruction*. Yes, Americans are sometimes slow to change and that's not all bad, but when we finally get it, we move faster and farther than any other nation in the world.

Again, Emily and her mother agree. Let's do it for them!

six

Crisis in American Education.

Jobs machine.
Our economy is not creating enough good paying jobs. This is due in part to the economic downturn of 2008. According to the U.S. Bureau of Labor Statistics, the United States had approximately 3,000,000 job openings in 2013, all waiting to be filled. In 2014 job participation finally showed a robust recovery, but lower paying positions led the rebound. This means many workers are losing ground, even when they are working. Eric Morath, "Jobs Return To Peak, But Quality Lags," *The Wall Street Journal,* June 7 – 8, 2014.

Inequality.
Of even greater concern is the "growing distance between the economically successful and those who have not or cannot begin to climb. The division has become too extreme, too dramatic, and static." Peggy Noonan, "Declarations, The Most Memorable Words of 2013," *The Wall Street Journal,* December 21 – 22, 2013.

"Today, we're spending almost $800 billion on 92 federal anti-poverty programs — and yet we have the highest poverty rate in a generation." Paul Ryan, "A Better Way Up From Poverty," *The Wall Street Journal*, August 16-17, 2014.

In 2014, French economist Thomas Piketty unveiled a theory tying capitalism to increasing inequality of income and wealth. Martin Feldstein disagreed. Feldstein, former chairman of the U.S. Council of Economic Advisers, believes the true problem in our economy is persistent poverty. He thinks we need "stronger economic growth and a different approach to education and training." Martin Feldstein, "Piketty's Numbers Don't Add Up," the Wall Street Journal, May 15, 2014.

A growing number of critics believe our educational strategies — or lack thereof — are major contributors to this crisis.

- "Just a quarter of U.S. public high school graduates possess the skills needed to succeed academically in college. That statistic should terrify this country, given the aggressive rise of economic competition and rapidly improving education elsewhere in the world. Left unchecked, we're slipping in the global race to sustain a quality workforce." Robert Trigaux, "How Go Gates' Big Bucks in Schools?" Perspective, *Tampa Bay Times*, April 27, 2014.

- **Low proficiency.**
  Arnie Duncan, U.S. Education Secretary says proficiency rates in public schools are lower than we realize. Some school districts have set low bars for proficiency in reading and math. "U.S. schools are failing tomorrow's labor force. Too few students are prepared with the skills they need to compete in a world-wide market and sustain American economic dominance. Economies grow by exploiting scarce resources, people most of all. The ultimate source of wealth is ourselves." Review and Outlook, "The Human Wealth of Nations," *The Wall Street Journal*, December 4, 2013.

- The 2011 National Assessment of Educational Progress revealed that only 35% of eighth graders perform at grade level or above in math. Rex Tillerson, "How to Stop the Drop in American Education." *The Wall Street Journal,* September 6, 2013.

- In 2011, the Scholastic Aptitude Tests showed that reading and writing scores were the lowest ever recorded. The ACT college entrance exam suggested that only 25% of high school graduates were ready for college.

- "Good high schools. Great faculty. Underperforming Students." That's a condensed version of recent education reports from Florida, spawned by an accountability system gone awry. Apparently, schools and teachers are doing great; it's just the students who aren't making the grade. "School Numbers Just Don't Add Up," Times Editorials: *Tampa Bay Times*, December 22, 2013.

- Will it help to toughen up standards in school and expect more from students? President Barack Obama and other political leaders have said the nation's long-term prosperity depends on fixing our high schools and preparing students to compete in a global economy. A study in 2010 found that the U.S. ranks at only number 12 in the percentage of adults ages, 25 to 34, who hold college degrees. President Obama has set a goal for the United States to become number one.

- While President Obama and most Americans of all political persuasions want equal opportunities for every student, advanced placement classes are limited to a small percentage of high school students. Ron Matus, "Poll: Make AP Open to All." *Tampa Bay Times,* October 25th, 2010.

Some statistics.
Now let's take a look at some statistics. These numbers come from *Statistic Brain.* Verification is through *Education Week, Children Trends Database:*

- High school students who drop out each day: 8,300.

- The percentage of students who repeat the ninth grade and go on to graduate: 15%.

- High school dropouts who commit crimes: 75%.

- Black dropouts who have spent time in prison: 60%.

- High school dropouts who are not eligible for U.S. jobs: 90%.

Statistics are one thing, but if we take a look at actual school performance, we may get a different perspective on what is happening. Perhaps our school standards are too high, but that's unlikely. Here are some questions from an eighth grade exam in 1912, Bullitt County, Kentucky. This was a research project under the auspices of the Bullitt County Genealogical Society.

- How many steps 2 ft. 4in. each will a man take in walking 21.4 miles?
- Diagram the Lord loves a cheerful giver.
- Through what waters should a vessel pass, going from England through the Suez Canal to Manila?
- Define cerebrum; cerebellum.
- Name five county officers and the principle duties of each.
- Name three rights given to congress by the constitution and three rights denied congress.
- Who settled the following states: Georgia, Maryland, Massachusetts, Rhode Island and Florida?
- Name the last battle of the Civil War; War of 1812; French and Indian War, and the commanders in each battle.

Hmm, maybe elementary school students didn't have it so easy in the old days! Is it more to the point to question whether students have it too easy today? The answer, of course, is that some students need more challenging assignments and other students need easier assignments and/or career studies.

Our misunderstanding of who people are, what they want, and how they can achieve their goals, has led to a blinkered strategy. Debate over school standards and Common Core Benchmarks are a result of this failed approach, because our standards and benchmarks are too high *and* too low. (Academic demands were too great for Emily and not sufficient for Jaylen).

It really depends on our students and their interests and abilities. The standards and benchmarks may be too high or not relevant to students "majoring" in career studies, and at the same time may be too low or not relevant for students "majoring" in college prep. Would it be a good idea to take a close look at our students and recognize their unique aptitudes and abilities? Yes, it would.

- **What about college?**
  Dr. Jeffrey L. Collier, psychology professor at South Carolina State University, believes that "college students arrive woefully academically unprepared; students study little, party much, and lack any semblance of internalized discipline; pride in work is supplanted by expediency. He states that the largest scam is that colleges have an incentive to retain paying students who have little chance of graduating. Jeffrey Collier, "We Pretend to Teach, They Pretend to Learn," Opinion, *The Wall Street Journal*, December 27, 2013.

- A survey of 9000 adults born in the early 1980s shows that only 32% of women had received a bachelor's degree by age 27 and only 24% of men. U.S. Bureau of Labor Statistics.

- Meanwhile, the Wabash Study of Liberal Arts Education found that student motivation actually declines over the first year in college. Surveys of employers reveal that only 25% of college graduates have the writing and thinking skills necessary to do their jobs. David Brooks, "$160,000 Too Much for an Empty Credential," *Tampa Bay Times*, April 23, 2012.

- Twenty-eight percent of Americans have a college degree. Elizabeth Behrman, "Nowhere Near Number One," *Tampa Bay Times*, July 6, 2012.

- The ACT College Entrance Exam results suggest that 25% of high school graduates are ready for college. Stephanie Banchero, "Reading, Writing, Scores Hit Low," *The Wall Street Journal*, September 15, 2011.

- According to Richard Vedder, Director of the Center for College Affordability and Productivity, "30% of the adult population has college degrees, yet the Department of Labor tells us only 20% or so of jobs require college degrees. We have 115,520 janitors in the United

States with bachelors' degrees. Why are we encouraging more kids go to college?" Lauren Weber, "Do Too Many People Go to College?" *The Wall Street Journal,* June 25, 2012.

- In 2012, the University of South Florida in Tampa, Florida, was criticized for a four-year graduation rate of 34%. Kim Wilmath, "USF Lambasted Over Its Graduation Rates," *Tampa Bay Times,* June 21, 2012.

- The State of Florida admitted that the graduation figures they supply include thousands of struggling students who transferred into adult education programs to earn a GED (High School Graduate Equivalency Diploma). Under the new formula, these GED students would not be included and this would result in a lower graduation rate. "Next year, Florida Won't Be Able to Hide Them." Ron Matus, *St. Petersburg Times*, December 13, 2011.

- Meanwhile, the NAEP (National Assessment of Educational Progress) exam is considered more objective and more valid than tests developed in most states. It designates a basic rating and a proficiency rating. Proficient means the student has a solid grasp of the material. In reading, 35 states set the passing bar for reading *below the basic level* on the NAEP. Massachusetts was the only state to set its bar for passing at the proficient level and that was only for fourth and eighth grade math tests. Stephanie Banchero, "States Failed to Raise Bar in Reading, Math Tests," *The Wall Street Journal, August 11, 2011.*

- Research showing that 75% of young men and women entering college do not receive adequate preparation for first-year courses is the catalyst for developing the Common Core standards. Jeb Bush and Joel Klein, "The Case for Common Educational Standards," *The Wall Street Journal*, June 24, 2011.

- All of these problems affect colleges and their graduates. Secretary of Education Arnie Duncan has proposed that colleges be measured by the gainful employment of the graduates and repayment of federal loans. But this would encourage universities to admit fewer students from low income backgrounds that must finance their education.

- It would also discourage graduates from pursuing important jobs that aren't lucrative. "Think of aspiring teachers and nurses, for example. If they're unlikely to earn sufficient money relative to their debt, they may struggle to find a college program willing to accept them." Bob Kerrey and Jeffrey T. Leeds, *The Wall Street Journal*, November 20, 2013.

My, how we are willing to go sideways instead of viewing our elephant head-on.

Well, this is certainly a mess. How can we possibly begin to sort out these problems when there are so many stakeholders, including parents, students, teachers, teachers unions —and some businesses that, however well-meaning, make money producing curriculum materials and technological teaching tools? Stir in politics and it makes for an unyielding and sometimes adversarial brew.

So only 25% to 30% of high school kids are ready for college and only 25% to 30% of college graduates have the writing and thinking skills needed for the job market. Why do these percentages keep coming up? Is there magic in the 25% to 30% figures? *Yes, there is.* And some of them involve doing the wrong thing harder. None of them acknowledge the great American myth or the one-size-fits-all strategy that has become a killing field for Emily and Jaylen.

seven

Magic: How Seeing the Elephant Changes Everything.

Yes, magic. Identifying the elephant does change everything. How does our destructive but friendly elephant get our attention? Much like a magician, she waves her magic wand and says abracadabra! Gads, now what do we see?

Keep in mind what the elephant's four sturdy legs include (academic achievement in the top 25% to 30% by the end of 8th grade, motivation, self-control, and the ability to focus). Let's briefly review chapter 6 and I'll add a few citations from appendix 1, which also deals with our current educational crisis.

- "Our Secretary of Education, Arnie Duncan reports a proficiency level in math in the state of Tennessee of 34%." Hmm. That's precisely the mental ability needed for advanced academic studies

- "Only 35% of eighth graders perform at grade level or above in math." Since we are now acknowledging the elephant, we expect that.

- "The ACT college entrance exam suggested that only 25% of high school graduates were ready for college." Not so shocking, once we see the elephant.

- "A survey of 9000 adults born in the early 1980s shows that 32% of women had received a bachelor's degree by age 27." Yep.

- "In Chicago, 40% of students drop out and only 8% of 11th graders meet college readiness standards." Eight percent is much too low, but recognizing the elephant makes us realize that not all high school students should go to college.

- "30% of students enrolled in community colleges nationwide complete their associate of arts degree on time, or graduate." That about right?

- "Each day, 8,300 high school students drop out of school." Not surprising when we see the elephant and realize we don't have sufficient advanced career or advanced academic programs geared to recognize unique abilities and individual differences.

- "A mother in Florida was aghast to find her son made a D and was still placed on the honor roll." If we let the elephant reconfigure our academic programs, there will be no need for an honor roll.

- "Parents strain so that their children can get to college and then end up learning— not much." Maybe they learn "not much" because they shouldn't be there in the first place. Sad.

- "Surveys of employers reveal that only 25% of college graduates have the necessary skills to do their jobs." There's that 25% - 30% bracket again, Ms. Elephant.

- "National average of Americans with a college degree is 28%." Okay, so what's the problem?

- "Colleges have lowered their standards in order to maintain enrollment." Yes, that's understandable, even if unethical.

- "Thirty percent of the adult population has college degrees, but only 20% of jobs require college degrees." Yep, yep.

- "The University of South Florida was criticized for a four year graduation rate of 34%." Too many unqualified students?

- "GED students are included as graduates to pump up graduation and scores." Once we recognize the elephant, we won't need GED programs.

- "Common Core is in response to 25% of students entering colleges not being adequately prepared." Of course, what's new?

- "A special six-week summer algebra Boot Camp in one school district because only 34% of ninth graders pass the end-of-course algebra exam." Our elephant says tusk! tusk!

- In May, 2014, the overall district passing rate in Florida came in at 38%." Hmm.

- The *Tampa Bay Times* reported that Florida "has good high schools, great faculties, but underperforming students." Apparently schools and teachers are doing great; it's just the students who are not making the grade. *Believe it or not, this can be true.* Students aren't making it because the bar has been set at a level that recognizes only the high academic IQ students, not the abilities and interests of the majority of students. In fact, this book is not about the "what" and the "why" but is mostly about the "who."

MAGIC!?

Wow! This little exercise sure seemed like magic. What was previously presented as "A Crisis in American Education" may be a crisis all right, but not the crisis we thought it was. But this isn't magic. No, it's a simple acknowledgment of the fact that the top 30% of achievers should go on to college. "And all the king's horses and all the king's men" won't change that. So is our problem solved? Should we just sit back and acknowledge the facts?

No, we still have a crisis in America. Not all of the top 30% are finding their way to college, and when they do, they aren't fully prepared for real college-level work. Meanwhile, the majority of students, those needing career studies, are left in the killing fields.

And on it goes. Maybe it's time to take off the eye mask and see the elephant. Maybe we need to acknowledge and celebrate the reality of differing human capacities and interests.

Jaylen and his parents would agree. So would Emily and her mother.

eight

What About other Opinions and Reforms?

Parent support.
Many teachers today will tell you that all these reforms are a waste of time because it's really the parents who are responsible for their students' poor efforts. They will give you a litany of negative experiences involving angry, recalcitrant, and aggressive parents, many of whom seem to have little interest in their children, and who don't follow school guidelines or read to their kids.

"I'm a teacher with 30 years of classroom experience at the seventh grade level," says Coleman Pont, "without the culture encompassing parental support, even the best teacher can fail. Principals tend to back parents when confronted with the fear of a parent going over their head to an even more scared administrator at the district office who is fearful of losing his job," Pont says. Letters to the Editor, *The Wall Street Journal,* September 27, 2010.

I agree with teachers such as Ponte. It's almost impossible to teach children when their parents are uncooperative and aggressive. But the teachers with negative views about parents usually work at schools where some of the best students — and their parents — have gone elsewhere — creamed off to a "better world." Once again, we are confronted with the elephant in the room, and some teachers are dealing with the academic coffee grounds after the cream has been siphoned off through the selective process.

But when you speak to teachers in one of the "Lake Wobegone Schools," where everyone is above average, whether it is a charter school, a magnet school, or a fundamental school, they will tell you how great and supportive parents are.

As we saw, Emily's mother and Jaylen's parents were cooperative, and we find many cooperative parents in all schools. But the preponderance of limited parental cooperation is found in the non-selective schools.

We need to keep trying to educate uncooperative parents, and some good has come from this, but trying to change the ingrained personalities and lifestyles of adults is not easy, even when they seek help. How do I know? I know because children, families, and adults came to my private practice for psychotherapy and were willing to shell out big bucks to change their personalities.

But even in intensive one-on-one counseling, with a well-trained professional, they almost always resisted change and wanted to cling to old, safe, but ineffective patterns of behavior. It's normal to want to maintain safe and comfortable personality patterns. Change is scary, especially when someone wants to tinker with who we are — or who we think we are.

Unfortunately, programs designed to help parents with their parenting skills seem to draw those who are already motivated, not the parents who are least cooperative. As a result, these programs end up "teaching to the choir."

Yes, disgruntled parents in a killing field's environment can be a huge problem, but a head-on assault to alter suspicious and negative attitudes just isn't feasible. The answer is to provide AAS and ACS programs that will engage and inspire students. When that happens, the cooperative parents will remain with their neighborhood schools. When they do, they will have a more positive effect on the negative parents than any seminars or courses provided by the school system.

In one killing field school only 3% of surveyed staff agreed that "parent support for this school is strong." Meanwhile, over at a selective (Fundamental) school, 100% of respondents said parents supported the school. Lisa Gartner, "Survey Shows School Woes," *Tampa Bay Times*, March 17, 2014.

Established reform programs

Turnaround process.
Florida state law mandates a turnaround process for chronically failing schools. Staff and sometimes even principals can be replaced. If the principal and teachers are unprofessional and uncaring, this might be helpful. But it is more likely that the failing school represents the residual "coffee grounds" and not the cream. Significant changes will not take place until the school is allowed to recognize brain and personality diversity and teach accordingly. That means career programs in addition to or instead of academic ones.

Preschool programs.
Preschool programs may help some students, although there are no solid data to support this. To be effective, these programs must include nutrition, healthcare, and family counseling in addition to academics. Intensive programs can produce some positive results in poor children, perhaps in the 10% range, but with no lasting effect on increased IQ scores.

In 2013, the Federal Department of Health and Human Services issued a comprehensive 346 page final report of its third grade follow-up to an ongoing Head Start impact study and found that while there were *initial* positive results, by the end of third grade there were very few impacts found in any of the four domains of health, cognitive, social-emotional, or parenting practices. OPRE report, October, 2012.

Ouch!

But we need to keep trying. We need to find ways to make initial achievement gains stick. This may not change abstract mental abilities, but higher achievement is a respectable goal as long as career education is an option along with college prep.

Sometimes I wonder if we should change the name of "Head Start" to "Catch Up." Even at age 4 and 5, poor kids don't have the advantages of upper-middle-class kids and it's difficult to catch up because the other kids, who are their upper-middle-class competitors, are continuing to progress at an even a faster rate.

An analogy comes to mind. If there is a super-duper race at the Indianapolis 500 Speedway and some folks are driving race cars while others folks are driving hot-rods assembled in their garage at home, it's going to be hard for the hot-rods to catch up to sleek, high-powered vehicles with professional drivers. I wish there were some way the hot-rodders could start the race early — a head start, but unfortunately human development is not similar to a racetrack.

Federal Housing Program.
Researchers from the University of Chicago, Harvard, and other institutions studied the effects of *Moving to Opportunity*, a federal housing program. In the 1990s it offered housing vouchers to more than 2000 low-income families. A separate control group with similar demographics did not move to a new neighborhood. The program aimed to boost education and income — but it largely failed. Participants who moved to better housing and safer neighborhoods showed only minimal economic or educational gains. Ben Cassleman, "Neighborhoods Confer Health, But Not Wealth," *The Wall Street Journal,* September 21, 2012.

Grading schools.
What about grading schools on an A to F scale? Florida teachers, superintendents, and school board members are questioning the value of the A to F grading system. Some have called for an end to this system, but more time is needed to make the transition to new exams, standards and expectations, especially with the introduction of Common Core. And automatic triggers can cause an entire school's grade to drop. An example is when fewer than 25% of students are reading at grade level. Jeffrey S. Solochek, "Curriculum," *Tampa Bay Times,* Dec. 19, 2013.

School Achievement Testing.
Most states use uniform achievement tests to measure and compare schools as well as teachers. At first blush, this seems to make sense, but what test is appropriate for every child? Indiscriminate testing of all students, regardless

of whether they are headed for college preparation or career training, results in inordinate pressure on students, teachers, and parents.

I can recall when low-achieving students were put on buses and sent on field trips on the day of the high-stakes testing. If the kids weren't in school on the testing day they weren't counted, and this had the effect of raising the school's overall test score. Alice in Wonderland? Maybe.

Many if not most answers to standardized test questions may be available in materials sent to schools by the test publishers, according to Meredith Broussard. Unfortunately, low income school districts can't afford to buy them. Meredith Broussard, "Why Poor Schools Can't Win at Standardized Testing," *The Atlantic Monthly*, July 15, 2014.

An unusual but scary example of rigidity resulting from mandatory testing of all children is the case of a child whose teacher made daily visit to assess his progress, even though he was in hospice care. He wasn't meeting his sixth-grade requirements because he was in a morphine coma and died three days after his mother objected to this process. The state responded by reaffirming that every child enrolled in public schools in Florida should have access to the best education possible "and measuring progress (*testing*) (author's insert) is the key to successful learning." Kathleen McGrory and Jeffrey S Solochek, *Tampa Bay Times*, Feb. 27, 2014.

While this is a dreadful example that we hope will not be repeated, I am reminded of a close friend who taught sixth grade in Madison, Wisconsin public schools. One of his special needs students had a full-time ESE teacher (special education associate) who sat in the classroom next to the special needs student and assisted the child with reading and writing. This student was significantly impaired and his low test scores pulled down the grade average for that class, which in turn affected the overall rating for the school. After experiencing displeasure from a school supervisor, the associate took it upon herself to *take the achievement tests for the child*. This resulted in excellent scores. Problem solved!

These state-mandated tests can help measure schools and teachers if they are reserved for college-bound students. Teacher and school comparisons would then be on an "equal playing field." At the present time they are tyrannical, because they are administered to the wrong persons at the wrong time. With the Elephant-in-the-Classroom model, career students would not be given state academic achievement tests. Why would they?

Today, we must teach to the test, and the test score itself can shape teaching priorities. For example, a test consultant could raise the class grade and thereby the school grade if a certain child, we'll call him Bryan, raised his math score by 10%. Bryan is already a pretty good student but has the potential to improve that score. Meanwhile, Celina is too far below the cutoff to affect the class and school assessment. It's unlikely that she can raise her score by 10% in just a few weeks. As a result, the consultant recommends giving Bryan extra help to improve his test score, leaving Celina where she is — lost. Can this really happen? Yes.

If educators believe these group achievement tests improve learning and accountability, let's continue to administer them. They measure academic achievement and should be given to students who are preparing for an academic future; not to students specializing in career and life skills.

Charter schools.
Charters are all the rage right now. Will they do the trick? It's too early to tell, but some of them seem to be doing well. And charters and vouchers stimulate competition. Neighboring public schools seem to improve because of competition with charters and "vouchered" private schools. Other charter schools may not be doing quite so well.

I'm reminded of a lawyer who told a psychologist that a new charter high school in Chicago had the answer to many of the school system's problems. It was receiving above-average grades from the state and graduating a high percentage of its students. The psychologist replied that he knew the school and didn't think it deserved an A grade. Why would he say that? *Here comes the elephant again.* The psychologist said what he said because he knew the school was creaming off the very best eighth-graders, so of course those students would do well in almost any school.

My thesis is that it doesn't matter if the school is for Black students, Hispanics, lower socio-economic kids, students from an inner-city school, or the well-off. If it selects the best students it will do well. *That old four-legged elephant is still in the room and having a mighty big impact* — and cream will always rise to the top. (This is true for advanced career study students as well as advanced academic study students).

Is there something wrong with taking students from an impoverished environment and offering them a good education? Of course not. Some students with excellent potential might be lost in a killing field's public school. It's a marvelous thing to ensure that students have a shot at a good future, whether that results from elite academics or elite career programs. But the fact is that many of these students of high academic potential would have succeeded anyway. So it's a very good thing to do, but it is not the solution for the majority of our kids.

Back in the 70s, my not-for-profit St. Petersburg Developmental Center received no government assistance but had sufficient revenue to hire a bus to provide free tutoring for poor students in the most deprived areas of our city. The only thing that slowed us down was that parents of some of these kids were afraid to allow our little bus to enter certain neighborhoods. They feared they were too dangerous. But we gave it our best effort and saw improvement in reading skills with many of these great kids.

No Child Left Behind.

Ten years ago, the United States Congress adopted *No Child Left Behind* legislation mandating that all students must be proficient in reading and math by 2014 or their school would be punished. Unfortunately, this legislation may have led to "teaching to the test" and an emphasis on remembering left-brain facts and details rather than critical thinking and creativity.

Miracle schools.

This push for higher achievement has led to accounts of miracle schools, but Diane Ravitch, former United States Assistant Secretary of Education, did some detective work that undermined these claims. One government official hailed the Bruce Randolph School in Denver, where the first senior class had a graduation rate of 97%. Wow! What happened to the elephant? That is indeed impressive. But, according to Ravitch, the schools ACT test scores were far below the state average. In its middle school, only 21% were proficient or advanced in math, placing the Bruce Randolph School at the 5th percentile or below 95% of other schools in Colorado. Only 10% of their students met state science standards.

The New Tech Network schools also claim high graduation rates. But again, there is a selective factor at work. We'd like to believe that our elephant has left the room, but that just ain't the case — not yet, anyway.

Also, according to Ravitch, Mayor Michael Bloomberg of New York reported an astonishing 49 point jump in fourth graders' scores at PS 33. In 2004 only 34% reached proficiency, but in 2005 83% made the grade. A year later, however, the proportion of fourth graders at PS 33 that passed the state reading test dropped 41 points. In 2010, 37% passed the test. Diane Ravitch, "School Miracle' Often Clever Sleight of Hand," *St. Petersburg Times*, June 2, 2011.

Gender – specific schools.

Neuropsychological studies continue to show significant brain differences between genders. Male brains utilize seven times more gray matter while female brains utilize ten times more white matter. Boys tend to over focus and are less sensitive to other people or their surroundings, while girls transition more quickly between tasks than boys do. We know that boys are more physically active and girls are able to sit still for longer periods of time.

It may be a good idea to educate boys and girls separately at some point in their development, but it still does not overcome the elephant's worry about selective factors. I worry about who will be invited to these schools or classes and whether they are academic or career oriented, or both? Larry Cahill, "Sex Differences in the Human Brain," *The Dana Foundation,* April 1, 2014.

Six-year high schools.
This model, which was rolled out in New York City and Chicago, requires *six years* of high school. Students graduate with not only a high school diploma, but also a college associate's degree. Some politicians, undoubtedly well-meaning, want to take that idea national. Rana Foroohar, "Time to Talk about the I Word," *Time Magazine,* February 10, 2014. In my opinion, this is an example of doing the wrong thing harder. Even though companies such as IBM and Microsoft have agreed to help design the curriculum, it's just too long and too late — and continues to support the ruinous "all kids are the same" and "all kids should go to college" mythology.

Virtual schools.
How about virtual schools? Can they save us? Florida virtual school leaders are proud of the high percentage of students completing their courses with a passing grade of 60 or above. But that figure doesn't reflect thousands of students who drop the courses within the school's 28 day penalty-free withdrawal period. In fact, 66% of students who enroll in a virtual course don't finish it. *Now we're back to the same percentage we see over and over again*: 34% complete the program and this is consistent with left brain, academic intellectual potential.

Based upon her teaching experience, Joyce Hicks, Associate Professor in the economics department at St. Mary's College, Notre Dame, Indiana, believes virtual classes are valid for searching and information gathering, but not as a stand-alone program. Students must be well-organized self-starters, and even then may have difficulties. She sees some positives, but believes it is a limited vehicle for collegiate level learning, in most cases.

In Minnesota, full-time online students in grades four through eight made as much progress in math in the 2009 –10 school year, measured by annual state exams, as their peers in traditional schools. But Ron Packard, CEO of an online company, acknowledged that achievement has declined at some schools. He thinks it's because more struggling students are registering for online courses. "They have become a school of last resort for many," he says. Stephanie Banchero and Stephanie Simon, "My teacher is an App," *The Wall Street Journal*, November 12 – 13 2011.

Despite mixed results, several states have *required* students to take on-line courses — whether they like it or not. I guess the term "academic freedom" doesn't apply to students and parents. Who's behind this? Educators who want to be on the cutting edge, or businesses that would like to help kids, but who are also motivated by profit?

The new school.
In a book by Glenn Harlan Reynolds, the author proposes the remaking of American education through charter and private schools combined with making the leap to online education. He points out that over 1.8 million K – 12 students are already receiving instruction online.

Donald R. Eastman, a highly-respected educator and President of Eckerd College in St. Petersburg, Florida, declared that the University of Florida online college is an ivory tower delusion. "The companies who are selling the snake-oil of disruptive innovation (Pearson, Coursera, Udacity, etc.) will make millions. The graduates of the University of Florida will have fellow alumni who paid much less for their degrees than they did, saw fewer real professors, and earned their degrees in their pajamas." Donald R. Eastman, "UF Online College an Ivory Tower Delusion," *Tampa Bay Times*, October 20, 2013.

Here's a comment from the person who identifies himself as *snopercod:* "When I attended engineering school, each of us had to learn how to set up and operate lathes and milling machines, weld with both a gas and electric arc, cast metal by several methods, bend sheet-metal, solder electric circuit boards, and various other hands-on disciplines. I'm having difficulty understanding how such things can be learned on the computer." http://legal insurrection.com/2014/01/review-the-new-school-by-Professor-Glenn-Reynolds/comment-page-1/# comment- 496212.

Virtual schools can and will help in career areas not requiring tool-making or the operation of heavy machinery, but it will take a few years of longitudinal research to determine the effectiveness of technology for teaching. (Please refer to Appendix 2 for a list of such occupations). Virtual schools help students who can't afford classroom participation or who are fully employed. They may also help students who have fallen behind or who need individualized learning, especially students with learning disabilities or other specific learning deficits. Virtual courses may help kids in ACS learn academic skills needed in the workplace.

New reforms

Graduation rates.
Graduation rates have become a government obsession. Get those graduation rates up and we'll solve all our problems. Right? Maybe not. In fact, a sharp increase in graduation rates is a symptom of our obsession with "pure" academics. This year, the high school graduation rate has topped 80% for the first time in U.S. history. Stephanie Simon, *Politico*, April 28, 2014.

This means that more high school students will receive a piece of paper (diploma) at graduation that does not represent career skills or a true college-prep education. Before we celebrate, we need huge gains in academic test scores and an enormous jump in elite technical and career certifications.

To support this assertion, we need only to look at what high school graduates are doing with their diplomas. Graduates are choosing work over college. Ben Casselman, "More High School Grads Decide College Isn't Worth It," *Heigh Ho*, April 22, 2014. Most of these students aren't prepared for college, and watered-down academic skills won't help them in the workplace. And a public school administrator told me that half of new enrollees in career programs at an outstanding community college are former college students.

Tutoring.
Tutoring promises help for students who are falling behind or who need individualized assistance. In Pinellas County, Florida, the school system is hiring college students at $20 an hour to tutor. The college students must have at

least a 2.5 grade point average. Bill Maxwell, "A Debate on Tutors, Teachers," *Tampa Bay Times*, December 15, 2013.

I'm a great believer in tutoring, and this is a good way to improve basic skills such as reading and mathematics. Experienced teachers would do a better job than college students and this approach won't change the basic thrust of teaching today, but I think it is a positive remedial effort.

Money.
Money (lots of money)! Another approach is simply the *massive infusion of money* into the elementary and secondary educational system. In 1985 a Missouri judge ordered the state to spend $2 billion over 12 years and per student funding increased to $25,000 per student. But the CATO Institute documented this effort, and a decade later student achievement hadn't improved. The judge admitted that spending all that money didn't accomplish much. Editorial: "Kansas Democracy Lesson," *The Wall Street Journal*, January 17, 2014.

I believe a heavy investment of money into our schools would do wonders if and when we sort out what we should be doing in public education. With the elephant still in the room, we are merely spending more money on the wrong things.

Scholarship programs.
A current example of monetary infusion is the Kalamazoo Promise. The Kalamazoo, Michigan program took a blind stance to family income levels, pupils' grades, and even to disciplinary and criminal records, thus becoming the most inclusive and generous scholarship program in America. Tuition and room and board to Michigan's public colleges, universities, and community colleges was paid for all students who started the program in kindergarten and completed high school.

Seven classes covered by *Promise* have graduated, but only a small percentage of students have received their college degrees so far. Some of the most troubling conditions confronting Kalamazoo children still exist: the pregnancy rate for Black teenagers in Kalamazoo is highest in the state. Only

44% percent of Black males graduate from high school. Ted C. Fishman, "The Tuition Jackpot," *The New York Times Magazine*, September 16, 2012.

This program is well-intentioned, as are most reform movements, and has helped a small number of students graduate from college in four years. It's much too early to evaluate the overall success of these kinds of programs, but it is unlikely they will make a significant difference except for the brighter and more motivated students, most of whom would have made it to college anyway. And the financial cost of the program is extraordinary.

Military schools.
These schools have been around for a long time. I attended one in Tulsa, Oklahoma. They offer structure and close personal attention. But again, these have been selective private schools. Now some charter schools are choosing to follow the military model in order to get more kids into college. Former San Francisco mayor Jerry Brown, who is now governor of the state of California, started the Oakland Military Institute in 2001. Other charter schools want to go military to replicate the instruction provided at Oakland Institute.

Military schools provide even more structure and self-control training than ordinary boarding schools, and they teach teamwork and willpower. Earlier I commented on research by Dr. Roy Baumeister at Florida State University which indicated that self-control is a key element for future success. Once again, this is a good effort, but if the goal is to get everyone into college, they're not listening to the elephant. Creaming is also a real concern. "School Goes Military to Push Kids to College," *Tampa Bay Times*, October 20, 2013.

College course reduction.
Since there will always be limited funding for state universities, especially during a recession, the Governor of Florida, Rick Scott, seems to be on a path that would force cuts to liberal arts courses such as anthropology and English as a way to increase funding for STEM (science, technology, engineering and mathematics) programs. Bill Maxwell, a writer for the Tampa Bay Times who has taught at the college level, believes this is a huge mistake. If this is in fact

true, I would agree with Mr. Maxwell. Bill Maxwell, "Requiem for College Life as I Knew It," Tampa *Bay Times*, Sunday, July 8, 2012.

The State of Florida is about to embark on an assessment of state colleges, including graduates' earning power, but will also add factors such as six-year graduation rates, the number of students in science and technology, and the percentage of graduates who get a job. This may inadvertently punish small colleges such as Florida A&M University, the state's historically Black public university. Tia Mitchell, *Times/Herald Tallahassee Bureau*, *Tampa Bay Times*, January 17, 2014.

Robin Mamlet, a former admissions dean at Stanford University, and Christine Van DeVelde, a journalist, raise the possibility of unintended consequences. They state that "in reducing college selection to a mere financial scorecard, the government is promoting a false value that has a high price indeed. "Should Colleges Be Factories For The 1%?" Robin Mamlet and Christine Van DeVelde, *The Wall Street Journal*, February 21, 2000.

Common Core.
This popular new approach is a set of K – 12 academic benchmarks that have been adopted by 45 states. Some folks had the impression that Common Core would demand college prep work for all students in high school. Therefore, my objection is that only 25% to 30% of students are capable and motivated to do well at that academic level.

Here's a quote from e-school news.com, December 9, 2013: "Students will be expected to take Common Core assessments in another year, making this academic year a critical time for schools to prepare. Many schools are starting to map their local curriculum to the Common Core State Standards and have begun teacher training and revision of their instruction plans to ensure these new standards will be integrated into teaching and learning across all curriculum areas — not just in English and math." If that isn't enough, they also have advice on how to "*train students' brains*" to help them learn these new standards better (author emphasis).

Yes, these massive reforms, which seem to occur about every five years, are intrusive and create confusion for teachers and administrators. Today in

Florida, for example, schools will be measured based on the new Common Core State Standards but their students will be taking the old state test which does not line up with Common Core benchmarks.

"Making matters worse, the talk in Tallahassee (Florida's Capitol) was of continued tinkering that could affect standards for years. State officials now want to revise the brand-new standards, and suddenly they are changing course on plans to replace the old FCAT" (former state test). Jeffrey S. Solochek, *Tampa Bay Times,* January 19, 2014.

But perhaps Common Core doesn't represent college prep work, after all. Professors from Stanford University and the University of Arkansas agree that children educated under Common Core will not be prepared to do competitive university work. Rather, it is geared for community college studies. Sandra Stotsky, a former member of Common Core's validation committee, is a professor emeritus at the University of Arkansas. She says the basic mission of Common Core is to provide students with enough mathematics to make them ready for a non-selective college — not for STEM.

Stotsky concludes that Common Core aims too low in mathematics and common core deficiencies also plague its English standards. She believes it does not prepare students for college majors in mathematics, science, engineering and technology- dependent fields. Sandra Stotsky, "Common Core Doesn't Add Up to STEM Success," *The Wall Street Journal*, January 3, 2014.

Diane Ravitch, well-known columnist and researcher, seems to agree with Stotsky. In a Twitter message to me on March 17, 2014, Ravitch complained that Common Core was not written by educators. She also believes it hasn't been thoroughly tested and "needs a major fix."

What to believe? If it is truly geared for high-level university academics, it will be over the heads of 65% to 70% of our students. If it is geared for community college, then the top 30% to 35% with high academic ability will be bored and frustrated and not well prepared for a rigorous four-year university education. This reform is a good example of what's wrong with our present system.

What's problematic with common core is that it is *common*. There is no such thing as a *common* child. All are different and all have unique characteristics, strengths and weaknesses. Gerald V. Bradley, "Common Concern for the Common Core," *The Irish Rover*, October 10, 2013.

The National Education Association (3 million member teachers' union) has supported Common Core, but has concerns about implementation. In a letter to National Education Association members, President Dennis Van Roekel stated that "in far too many states implementation has been completely botched. Seven of ten teachers believe implementation of the standards is going poorly in their schools." Bob Bluey, *The Heritage Network,* March 1, 2014.

Parent Trigger.
We spoke of this previously as one response to negative and aggressive parents. One of the most radical reforms now underway, this program would transfer power from education officials and teachers' unions to parents. *Parent Trigger* mandates that failing schools may be taken over by students and parents and reorganized to become more effective. Parent Trigger became California law in January, 2010. According to David Feith, schools are eligible for triggering if they fail to make adequate yearly progress for four consecutive years. When the California law was passed, 1,300 of California's 10,000 schools qualified for the Parent Trigger Program.

Can Parent Trigger help reform schools? It may be of some help, but it may also be disruptive. Do parents have the time, knowledge, and resources to improve their children's school? Are the teachers' unions and school administrators really responsible for each failing school? My thinking is that it won't make much difference who is running the school as long as the current system is maintained, a system that actually breeds core pockets of school failure. I refer to these schools as the killing fields, because children are not selected for advanced collegiate *or* career studies.

Mastery.
A national movement to base grades on mastery of the subject and not homework or behavior has gained some traction. Educators went to this approach when they discovered that nationally 26% of high school seniors met college benchmarks in four important subjects. (There's that 25% to 35% figure again)! With the mastery approach, homework is not graded and student's can retake portions of tests. It's too early to assess this program but the approach suggested in this book would solve the problem of not meeting benchmarks. Kids in career studies wouldn't need academic benchmarks because they would be on a mastery-based program. "Students Have One Assignment: Learn." *St. Louis Post Dispatch,* December 29, 2013.

Teacher transfer.
Another controversial approach is teacher transfer. In the Miami, Florida public schools, low performing teachers were transferred involuntarily to different schools. What happened? Students in the affected schools received new teachers and began to perform at higher levels, according to achievement test scores. Sadly but predictably, students in the schools where the low performing teachers were transferred began to have lower scores.

But teachers and teachers' unions are not happy about forcing teachers who are suspected of low-average performance to transfer to other schools. Critics worry that just transferring low performers won't improve the quality of the system as a whole. Bill Maxwell, "Teacher Transfers as a Tool, *Tampa Bay times*, December 1, 2013.

I would like to take this opportunity to say something in defense of our teachers and our public school system today. Comparing our kids with kids in Norway, China, or other foreign countries is ludicrous, in my humble opinion. This is truly comparing apples and oranges. America is an immigrant society that accepts and works with people from all socio-economic levels. Students in our top 30% to 35% of academic ability and interest do as well as similar children in other countries. *This isn't about a race to the moon.* This is about giving all American children an opportunity to be successful, contributing citizens.

Wei Luo is CEO of the Cal Sunshine Education Center in Claremont, California. He reports that the higher students score on PISA (Program for International Student Assessment), the lower those students score on self-confidence and entrepreneurship. So the fact that U.S. scores lag in global tests may not be such a bad thing.

Matthew Muller said visiting Chinese students reported that they had 12-hour school days at a Beijing high school, followed by homework. This obviously left them with less time for athletics and social interaction, compared to US students. Wendy Kopp visited rural schools in China, and noted that fewer than 30% of rural Chinese students make it to high school, where they would participate in the PISA exam. *So much for comparing apples and oranges!* Wendy Kopp, (op-ed) "Let's call off the Education Arms Race," *The Wall Street Journal*, December 4, 2013. There's that 30% figure again! I know I'm getting repetitious but it keeps cropping up, doesn't it?

My own tour guide in China told me that his mother locked him in his bedroom for three weeks prior to the federally-mandated high-stakes achievement test. Except for food and bathroom breaks, he was there to cram. And cram he did.

This concludes our review of most of the reform movements out there. Once we discovered the elephant in the room, it became clear why these concepts and plans won't help much. They don't recognize the killing fields and how selection has reshaped the system. Non-college-bound kids are not getting career training and parents and politicians still insist on college for everyone.

I'm afraid most of these reforms aren't much help to Emily and Jaylen.

nine

How the Elephant's Plan Changes Things.

Shakeup the status quo?
Will the Elephant-in-the-Classroom movement shakeup the status quo? You bet. What impact will it have on students, teachers, and current programs? Will we still have behavior problems, absenteeism, and drop-outs? Yes, but I suspect that students who have dropped out physically or psychologically will fall from approximately 40% to below 5% of the school population. That's because students will find the work relevant and interesting — and maybe even financially profitable, while they're still in school.

Effect on Current Reform Groups.
What about vouchers and tax-exempt scholarships? We should see a continuation of their growth, although parents will enjoy greater satisfaction with their public school system than in the past. That's because one of the drivers of private school enrollment is parental desire for structure and safety. If we ride the elephant, there will be less need for students to go A.W.O.L. or act out in the classroom. Vouchers, scholarships, and charter schools will always be in demand. In addition, I suspect some of these voucher and charter schools will emphasize the AAS (advanced academic studies) approach, while others will emphasize the ACS (advanced career studies) approach. More power to them.

Teach the test.
Will teachers still be tempted to continue to "teach to the test?" If the government continues to use testing to evaluate teachers and schools and wants AAS students to compete with Norway and China, and a slew of other countries, then teaching to the test might continue, but it won't be necessary. These students

will be capable of true university work and they will be motivated to progress at a rapid pace similar to students in current pre-Cambridge, gifted-child, and International Baccalaureate programs.

Those who think teaching children is similar to the Olympics, where a tiny number of athletes are over-trained in order to maintain the prestige of the nation, needn't worry. The new AAS will assure superior rankings among nations and will handle any tests thrown their way.

Teachers, instructors, and role models in the ACS program will have no need to fall into the testing trap, because much of the work their students and apprentices accomplish will not be amenable to large-scale standardized achievement tests. Instead, they will be evaluated based on work produced. A good example is making a hammer, much as I did in my high school shop class. My performance evaluation was based on how the hammer looked, how well it worked, and how long it took me to make it, not on a paper-and-pencil test.

ACS kids will be freed from what they perceive to be a rat race and instead will be challenged to create, innovate, and learn skills that will reward them with income and self-esteem. There will be an increase in excited, motivated kids. This is what poor Emily missed out on.

ADHD

Fewer young people will be diagnosed with ADHD. While the American Psychiatric Association estimates the incidence of ADHD at 5% (*Center for Disease Control, 2012*), community samples reveal an incidence of 11% overall and 13.2% for boys. In my opinion, this inflated diagnosis is the result of the killing fields. We're not allowed to match our teaching to the students' interests and abilities, and children often receive this diagnosis because of parent and teacher pressure.

ACS will allow for movement and hands-on skills, not quiet passivity, and college-bound students won't be bored by non-challenging work. ADHD type behavior is much more frequent in males than females, and some of this may be attributed to boys' apparent greater need to move in space and enjoy physical activity.

A recent study showed that 30 minute sessions of aerobic activity before school helped young children with symptoms of attention deficit hyperactivity disorder. Sumathi Reddy, "Exercise Helps Children with ADHD in Study," *The Wall Street Journal*, Sept. 9, 2014.

I believe the incidence of ADHD will return to the 1970's and 80's valid levels of 3% to 4%. As a result, much less stimulant medication will be prescribed as well.

Gender.

What will be the effect on gender? Under our present system, both genders suffer. Feminist Camille Paglia reminds us that there has been "a war against boys. Primary school education is a crock, basically. It's oppressive to anyone with physical energy, especially guys." She points to the example of schools cutting recess. "They're making a toxic environment for boys." Bari Weiss, "A Feminist Defense of Masculine Virtues," *The Wall Street Journal*, December 28 – 29th 2013.

Job participation for women has rebounded since the 2008 recession but employment for males has lagged behind previous levels. Why? Women have tended to hold jobs in health, education, hospitality, and retail, all sectors that have weathered the economic turmoil in recent years. Male dominated sectors such as construction and manufacturing have suffered the brunt of the recession. Men lost more than 6 million jobs in the recession and its aftermath, while women lost 2.7 million jobs.

ACS will allow and encourage male students to enter these recession-proof occupations dominated by women, and female students will flow into construction and other previously male-dominated employment positions, based on their interests and skills.

Jonathan House interviewed a 33-year-old woman who tried to switch from social work to carpentry, but it was a difficult transition. Many women report a lack of labor mobility and difficulty breaking into the traditional male-dominated fields. According to House, women are often not taught or encouraged to participate in jobs such as electrician, plumber, or builder. Jonathan House, "Record Number of Women in the Workforce," *The Wall Street Journal*, November 18, 2013.

Some fathers do not encourage their daughters in these areas and schools only occasionally offer these opportunities. This will change with the ACS model, which will offer hands-on experience along with instructors and role models to engage any student, regardless of gender, to work in activities they enjoy and are good at.

Discipline.
There'll be fewer discipline problems. Overall, classroom behavior will improve and the incidence of bullying will decrease. ACS kids will be kept busy with challenging and relevant work, while college-bound kids will be challenged rather than insulted by boring, tedious academic assignments. Safety and improved school morale will slow the flight of children to private schools. It will also improve teacher morale. At the present time, 50% of those entering the teaching profession leave within five years. Susan Moore Johnson, Director, Harvard University's Project, "The Next Generation of Teachers," *Education Week*, WEBINAR, April 29, 2014.

Bullies are often kids with low self-esteem who are embarrassed because of their poor academic performance compared to high academic achievers. ACS will offer real-world challenges and keep these right-brainers busy with hands-on activities. As the Catholic nuns used to say, "Idleness is the devil's workshop."

Crime.
The prison population will be significantly reduced. Since students will have marketable skills and attitudes of pride forged in the technical and job arenas — as well as some money in their pockets — they will be much less susceptible to negative peer-group pressure and criminal activity.

We are all concerned about the tragedy in Furguson, Missouri. In my opinion, that fatal confrontation was the result of more than racial attitudes. The unemployment rate for young Blacks remains twice that of young

Whites, and "Just 5% of African-American students meet the ACT's college readiness benchmarks." *Pew Research Center and Bureau of Labor Statistics.* White and Black kids in poverty need to be identified earlier for advanced courses in academic studies or career studies. They need to be taking college prep courses or learning career skills that lead to good paying jobs and self respect.

Immigration is an obvious analogy. If children who are on the outside looking in are given new opportunities for good paying jobs and self respect, *their* children and grandchildren will more easily adapt to the mainstream of American life.

Better balanced.
Students will be better-rounded. "Over the last 15 years the following classes have declined, and in some schools eliminated: instructional time, recess, science fairs, field trips, art, music, debate, speech, creative writing, academic and vocational electives, and the joy of learning." "Florida Schools Moving in the Right Direction," April 10, "Commentary," *Tampa Bay Times*, April 15, 2014.

The elephant's plan will allow for all of these important activities. Because of the concentrated nature of this encapsulated group, AAS students will also have time for one career option, as well as many of the above activities. Jaylen may find he has acting ability, for example. This mirrors the elite universities that now have shorter academic years. And ACS students will not be burdened by esoteric academic courses and the state and/or federal testing that drives them.

AWOL.
There will be fewer dropouts. Students who drop out of high school without skills and often drift into criminal activity will be something for the history books. Now students may wish to drop in, rather than drop out; drop in to career education that is *relevant* to their lives and futures. Some adolescents might want to enter the workforce early, but they will have the skills, attitudes and experience to give them an opportunity for financial success.

Sure, a few kids will come from such dysfunctional homes or harbor such severe oppositional traits that they are unable to function in any academic or work environment. In my opinion, this shouldn't make up more than a tiny percentage of the population, and public and private behavioral and therapeutic schools will continue to offer rehabilitation to prevent total failure.

Failing.
Grade retention will be a thing of the past. AAS students will be prepared for advanced academic material and students in ACS will not progress by grade level but rather through achievement of a series of individual certifications at their neighborhood school location, as well as county career centers and community college programs. This will lead to concrete productivity and certificates of accomplishment. Completion of several years of training will lead to an ACS high school diploma, and this diploma will carry much greater weight in the world of work than a regular academic high school diploma. They will also receive instruction in reading and math to enable them to understand the manuals and directions that are necessary for I.T. and other career work these days.

All of this will be accomplished through classroom work, tutoring, distance-learning, and educational electronic games. No child will be left behind and there will be no need for a NO CHILD LEFT BEHIND program. We will also see the end of the GED (graduate equivalency degree) which is designed to help under-performing students, but is also used to improve graduation rates.

Spawning new programs.
Examples of the types of programs that will develop and flourish are found in a high school in Florida that now offers classes in piloting, spaceflight and aeronautical science. Clearwater High School in Clearwater, Florida, has established a partnership with the Embry-Riddle Aeronautical University. "This high school started a 'wall-to-wall' academy concept last year in which all students take classes in career-themed areas such as business, science, technology, fine arts and hospitality. Students can earn industry certifications giving them a path directly to work." *And students can earn a pilots license by the time they complete the program.* Cara Fitzpatrick, "School Program Takes flight," *Tampa Bay Times*, November 29, 2013.

Our elephant has big ears and would love to fly. She'd like to see similar programs in all high schools.

Spur economic growth.
According to William A. Galston, economics writer for *The Wall Street Journal,* "Our labor force is in the process of shifting from an era of rapid expansion to much slower growth. This will cause U.S. economic growth to fall from its historical average of 2.17% per capita annually (1929-2007) — to half that level or less in coming decades." He believes we need to do more to encourage labor force participation by helping to ensure young adults receive meaningful training in skilled trades, many of which now face labor shortages. William A. Galston, *The Wall Street Journal,* December 11, 2013.

The Elephant-in-the-Classroom model will result in effective career training at the high school level and greater participation in community college academic and career programs, resulting in less teen unemployment. This is especially true for those who are overlooked in our present system: poor youngsters who have been deprived of early enrichment and kids from single-parent homes.

The push has been for more kids to go to college. The elephant's program will actually put more *qualified* kids in college than the current program. Students with the ability and motivation for college will be better prepared and should obtain more scholarships, while the number of career students will attend community colleges for both career and academic studies. So even if we have "college on the brain," this is the way to go.

Right, Emily and Jaylen?

ten

Marketing the Elephant.

Selling career education.
We'll need a full scale marketing blitz to increase the acceptability of career education and to counter the myth that college is always the superior outcome. This marketing could feature successful role models, including celebrities from business, the arts, and occupations such as race car drivers, and baseball and soccer All-Stars.

One such role model, at least for parents and grandparents, is John Ratzenberger, who played the part of Cliff Clavin on the 1980's sitcom "Cheers." He's promoting the restoration of shop classes in U.S. high schools. Another entrepreneur, Jack Buscher, has funded a skilled "trade ambassador" to walk the halls of local high schools to recruit teenagers into career fields. Josh Mandel, "Welders Make $150,000? Bring Back Shop Class," *The Wall Street Journal,* April 22, 2014.

How about acknowledging non-college people who have developed successful local businesses and who are making an excellent income? Marketers and advertisers in the business world could assist in developing a plan. How about Selena Gomez, and Harry Styles of *One Direction*, writing a song or giving ACS a plug at their concerts?

ACS students could create videos and presentations for younger students and their parents who are considering ACS. How about some friendly competition with AAS via T-shirts labeled "We Work For A Living," "ACS Students Have More Fun!" and "We'll Fly It, We'll Drive It, And We'll Own It."

Most of the marketing outlined above is primarily for parents, politicians and school administrators. *Students themselves won't need to be sold on a system that is interesting, relevant, and gives them hope for the future.* Once students experience career success, word-of-mouth will go viral. But how do we get parents and grandparents to see that career education opens doors rather than closing them?

Cost factors.
What will pull parents and students to ACS? There should be no student or parent fees for public school career training, and students may be able to put money in their pockets at age 16 or 17 rather than at age 22 or 23, which is often the case with students today who struggle through college. It cost about $120,000 (loans, tuition, plus the cost for leaving the workforce for 4-5 years) to pursue a college education. Mark Peters and Douglas Belkin, "Bachelor's Degree Payoff Can Seem Elusive," *The Wall Street Journal*, June 25, 2014. And that six-year difference between age 24 and age 17 represents 29% of the 24-year-old student's life at that time!

Let's remember that undergraduate loans alone are in the neighborhood of $30,000 and yet the February – March 2014 Gallup Poll of 30,000 college graduates showed that only 4% of those with an undergraduate debt of $30,000 were thriving in their work environment.

In addition to saving a bundle of money, bragging rights for ACS students will come from living in the real world, expanding areas of the brain that aren't stretched in AAS, and walking in the shadows of places like Georgia Tech and MIT. These are young people who want to "mix it up" in an historic American fashion rather than follow elitist footsteps. ACS will focus on attainment of specific and usable skills rather than academic test scores.

Hey, maybe potential ACS kids such as our Emily are the innovative kids — the truly brainy kids — if one considers attributes other than those found in the somewhat narrow academic brain. These folks are open to creative, social, and hands-on work that may result in a greater income than that of the AAS student and certainly greater income than most of the children who today are forced to follow a general education path and end up dropping out, either officially or psychologically, and then facing low self-esteem and minimal jobs with minimal pay.

Creativity.
This program will stimulate creativity and innovation, bulwarks of American commerce. Learning history and Shakespeare at a four-year college is valuable and broadens our society, but right-brain and higher brain centers may be more stimulated by *active* learning that involves technology and problem solving. We know the brain is plastic and that our experiences influence mental ability. Circus jugglers and London cab drivers who use maps show brain changes linked to these practices.

In time, ACS will not be viewed as a lesser option then AAS. In some ways it will lead to better results and in some ways it will not. Much of this is in the eye of the beholder and will depend on the programs drawn up by local school boards and administrators, along with the values and interests of students themselves.

ACS students will need to boast about their programs; what they have learned, and how much money they're making. And yes, they'll need a full range of athletics and competition on the playing field, along with the AAS folks. I predict that these right-brainers will do very well against the academic types. Not only will the ACS students do well on the athletic field, they may surprise some folks in shared knowledge and creativity. Maybe they'll even challenge AAS students to debates.

No way, you say; the AAS kids would embarrass the ACS kids. Yes, when it comes to questions about the great books, Aristotle, and the meeting of modernity, AAS kids may sweep the field. But what happens when there is tune identification or estimates of the square footage of the room where they are sitting for their debate, drawing a picture of someone in the audience, making a hammer, taking a small engine apart, composing a song on the spot or creating a funny story about a banana and a cherry, or leadership questions such as eight people in a lifeboat where there is only room for six and sufficient provisions for two?

What then?

So, different kinds of intelligence lead to differing capabilities and interests. Do we need all types? You bet. We need great philosophers and economists. We also need great technicians and the workers who make things run — and courses that fit their needs.

There are other models being developed across the country. One with promise is MTI, which stands for Marion Technical Institute. It is located in Ocala, Florida. MTI is pretty nifty sounding, wouldn't you say (An MIT for working folks)? Their approach is to take only juniors and seniors, and incoming students must be 16 years of age or older. Students have most of their academic work out of the way and spend the last two years of high school earning certifications as well as high school and college credits.

Unfortunately, students at MTI can't just focus on functional academics tied to their career specialties. They still need to worry about comprehensive academics, including Spanish and chemistry. But thankfully, the school itself is exempt from the Florida Department of Education's grading system because of its small size and lack of 10th grade-tested students. There is also no year-end state evaluation, but this school is doing better than most schools in terms of completion rate and achievement scores. Unfortunately, selection is again a factor, because private transportation is required to get to school. But I think another reason for the school's success is the relevance of its offerings.

MTI is supported in part by local companies and professional associations: Automotive technology is sponsored by the Ford Motor Company of Ocala, building services are sponsored by the County Builders Association, business and finance are sponsored by Gateway Bank, Career Academy cooperation is through the College of Central Florida, culinary arts is sponsored by Cheney Brothers, legal studies are sponsored by the Marion County Bar Association, production and design technology is sponsored by Lockheed Martin and R&D Manufacturing, information technology is sponsored by CenturyLink.

These folks have captured the spirit I'm referring to. They are proud to wear T-shirts sporting their motto "Where Education Meets Experience" outlined in the school's colors of navy-blue and gold. Oh, and their mascot? *Pioneer*. Perfect.

Some ACS students and trainees will decide to attend college. If they go to college and are successful they will need to put in a plug for their ACS alma maters, as well as the universities they may subsequently attend. Others will pursue academics in a more gradual fashion as they move along, taking advantage of access to libraries and online courses, or returning to post-high school programs at ages 30, 40, 50, or later.

During the Second World War, large numbers of students attended career schools to assist in the war effort. The Samuel Gompers School in San Francisco taught students aircraft maintenance, welding, and a number of other critical skills. No one dared ridicule those students. I think that's because the goal was a patriotic one. The reason some people look down on career-oriented students today is that these programs are, by and large, too little too late and not well coordinated. And career-oriented students are still forced to struggle with classroom academics and high-stakes testing instead of earning certifications relevant to their future.

But it's time to drop our ancient prejudices for passive learning and memorization over active learning. Sorry, Aristotle! Thank you, Leonardo Divinci! Leonardo couldn't afford college and shamefully described himself as "not being a man of letters."

Emily isn't a woman "of letters" either, but with guidance and expert training she might have surprised us all.

eleven

What will the Elephant's Plan Cost?

What will it cost?
Those readers who acknowledge that awareness of brain function points us in new directions might be wondering who will pay for this remarkable program. *They should be concerned!* In 2014 it is estimated that our government at all levels, federal, state, and county, will spend over $985 billion on education. By comparison, we will spend $832 billion on the military defense of our country.

But apparently not all of that money is spread out equally among public schools, at least at the elementary level. Peggy Noonan reported in *The Wall Street Journal* that the *Washington Post's* Susan Edelman visited public school 106 in Far Rockaway, NY to find no gym or art classes, while the library was "a junk room." The nurse's office lacked essentials and there were no math or reading books for the Common Core Curriculum. Kids were left to watch movies and kindergartners were taught in dilapidated trailers. The principal frequently missed work or came in toward the end of the school day. Peggy Noonan, "Our Selfish Public Servants," *The Wall Street Journal*, January 18 – 19, 2014.

Sounds like the killing fields, doesn't it? Most of these examples of failure are from poor neighborhoods. The euphemistic term for these inner-city schools is "high need" or "Renaissance" schools. In one of these schools, in Tampa, Florida, parents don't come to meetings unless food is provided. Only 16% of third-graders passed the state reading test last year. Marlene Sokol, "A Long Road," *Tampa Bay Times,* March 23, 2014.

In the past few years, the federal government's educational spending, including Pell Grants and veterans' benefits, accounted for $94 billion. Recently, that spending has increased to $145 billion per year. According to *The Wall Street Journal*, the United States as a whole spends $115,000 per student for education. And not all Pell Grant and student loan money is used as intended. At Colorado Mesa University, there is concern because some students took out an average of $25,000 in student loans, ditched classes, and used the money for other purposes (Pell Grant money can be used for non-educational purchases). Emily Shockley, "CMU hopes to Cut Student Loan Debt, fraud," *GJ Sentinal.com*, Dec. 29, 2013.

At the local school district level, school boards report expenditures of between $6000 and $7000 per pupil per year, but these figures do not include capital expenses and other items. A true cost is probably closer to $12,000 – $14,000.

Is $115,000 enough? It depends on whether or not it gives us what we want. And what we want are happy creative citizens who will help our economy grow. If we are sure of the outcome, we would spend twice the current amount and still be happy — wouldn't we?

So we're already spending a lot of money. Will we need to raise more money? Making career studies available on a much larger scale will incur additional costs, but I believe that more Americans, especially our business community, will be willing to allocate funds and even agree to tax increases if they know the program makes sense and is working. At the same time, I believe this redirection and clarification of goals will result in savings that can be used for the AAS and ACS programs.

The bottom line is that the money we invest in education will continue to follow the student, whether that student is in a super-academic or super-career program. Monies will follow the students and teachers as they move from the general classroom population to ACS to help pay for a first class, elite-career program — and to strengthen and expand the AAS program as well.

Some of the structure is already in place, needing only a change in the perception of what students need and the coordination of those services. In Pinellas County, Florida, for example, we have limited career programs in high schools, as well as middle-school magnets offering some technology. We have a long-established county technical program, although some of the equipment and teachers are in the local community, and some are in another city. Sometimes private fees are required for post-high school career programs and this discourages the very students we want to prepare for the world of work. And I suspect this violates the concept of a free public education.

Community college.
We have some legislators who are catching on to the need for more choice of services and we have reform measures such as the New York City program mentioned earlier. Pinellas County, Florida, has a broad community college career program and a private educational foundation that raises money for all school programs, including career education.

Community colleges are essential to meaningful reform. Even though many community colleges have expanded to four-year programs, their core mission is two-year degrees and career training. In this way, they focus on meeting the needs of local employers and not duplicating university offerings. Some of the community colleges have been criticized for expanding their four-year programs, but this can help accommodate students who have the ability and motivation for advanced academic work, but who cannot afford to attend a state university.

Private foundations.
Private educational foundations will be necessary to involve the private sector and develop Elephant-in-the-Classroom strategies. In Pinellas County, Florida, Dr. Gus A. Stavros founded the Pinellas Education Foundation in 1986. His group has raised more than 110 million dollars to support students and teachers. The vision of this group is that "every student will be prepared for life after school, whether that choice is to attend college, enter the workforce, or obtain technical training."

And at the post-high school level, let's not forget private-for-profit technical schools. There are approximately 150 institutes offering courses such as nursing, criminal justice, business information technology, and other programs to over 60,000 students. Students are borrowing lots of money to pay for these programs, and their very existence is evidence that we need more career training in our public school system. Gretchen Morgenson, "Inspecting a Student Loan Spigot," Sunday Business, *The New York Times*, January 19, 2014.

Dozens of private coding "boot camps" have sprung up to teach programming languages such as Python and Ruby on Rails. These coding schools last from 8 to 12 weeks, cost from $10,000-$15,000, and have job placement rates of 82% to 99.2%. Melissa Korn and Lauren Weber, "Coding Schools Tone Down Rosie Jobs Script, *The Wall Street Journal*, May 21, 2014. Once again, these are the types of career skills that should be taught in our public school system beginning in middle school. Otherwise, poor kids will be left out in the cold.

Some government officials want to clamp down on for-profit schools because they account for a high percentage of student loans, although 15% of borrowers at community colleges default compared to 13.6% at for-profit schools. These for-profits may serve a larger share of older and poorer workers who are unable to pay for a four-year college. "Review and Outlook," *The Wall Street Journal*, March 22 – 23, 2014.

A different approach is Wisconsin's Fast Forward Initiative. It lets employers, rather than the state, develop job-training programs. Employers apply for state grants and train workers in the skills they need. So far, the state has approved $1.4 million to train manufacturing workers, $1 million to train customer service workers, and up to $300,000 to train construction workers. Fifteen million dollars is currently available for employer-led training of workers.

Business and philanthropy.
If the Elephant-in-the-Classroom approach is to work, it will need unprecedented support from private industry. Companies need to contribute monies

to the local school system, ear-marked for career training and apprenticeships. They will also need to coordinate with schools to develop working models.

I suspect that even the conservative business community will not object to an increase in taxes for career studies, if necessary. One nice thing about career work is that it is less of a political football. Whereas liberals and Tea Party folks are on opposite sides of debates about school financing and curriculum content, they will all agree that making a soufflé requires mostly the same steps and skills that it always has, and won't be arguing about curriculum materials — or recipe books.

The "Year Up" crash course program developed for disadvantaged students, some of whom have only GED degrees, shows that private industry has its heart in the right place. These programs provide six months of intensive training followed by six months of internships with Fortune 500 companies including J.P. Morgan Chase and American Express. Students are given stipends of a few hundred dollars per week. The funds could be docked if students don't adapt to the social codes and norms of the workplace, such as showing up late for work. "Year Up," CBS *60 Minutes*, January 26, 2014.

Next Generation?
An outstanding example of support from business is the Ford Motor Company *Next Generation Learning Communities* that have set out to establish career academies at the high school level with the goal of helping all students become college and career ready. *Next Generation* is real-world and performance-based. It redesigns secondary schools to permit career study programs for all students and encourages community involvement in student projects. This looks like a winner! *Fordngl.com*.

Endowed institutions such as the Gates Foundation could make a major impact by investing money in career education. In the past, they have emphasized teacher training and Common Core Benchmarks rather than altering the one-size-fits-all — all kids are the same — strategy of our government.

It's true that increases in school board budgets have not always led to effective change, but with the Elephant-in-the-Classroom concept we're talking about career development that directly affects future employees. I believe private industry will stand up and be counted!

On the AAS side, we already have gifted programs, including public charter schools for the gifted, advanced placement programs, International Baccalaureate programs, and the challenging pre-Cambridge programs (creaming that recruits a good number of the collegiate strivers).

Savings.
Happy, enthusiastic kids in both the AAS and ACS programs will result in fewer nursing stations and fewer personal problems requiring counseling. Some counselors will gravitate to ACS where they will help children find a career path and ensure they receive reading and math skills necessary for their certifications. *Could we really do away with on-campus police personnel?* Yes, we could — in many settings. Nothing will return private school parents to the mother ship faster than a safe ship with multiple destinations!

Anyone who has worked with children and adolescents knows that they often communicate nonverbally. When they are unhappy they may not say much, but you can see it in their behavior. A good number of these youngsters are bored and frustrated in school. They may not admit it and may laugh it off in public or become the class clown. It's easier to make fun of the system than to admit to feeling stupid. When kids cut school or are absent because they say they're not feeling well, it's often because they just don't want to be there.

Emily and Jaylen understand that. Why can't we?

twelve

Why Do We Refuse to See the Elephant?

Why don't we get it?
Our students don't believe what they're doing is relevant to them or to their future lives. We need to prepare the child, based on that child's strengths, weaknesses, and special attributes, to find employment, live the good life, support our country, and become a role model for other students. For most students that future won't include a classic, liberal arts college experience. Are we being soft if we design life preparation to fit the strengths and weaknesses of each youngster? Are we giving up on our kids? No, we will be advancing our kids in the best way possible.

Our present system is not causing problems at just the high school level; it is creating problems at the university level as well. But with the Elephant-in-the-Classroom approach advocated here, universities will have fewer students overall, and expensive remedial courses necessary to salvage kids who don't belong there will cease to exist. At the present time, there are too many students in college who are not benefiting from the coursework offered, or the coursework has been watered down to enable them to graduate — *somehow* (and eventually).

And since there is a surplus of graduates available, they are now taking some of the jobs that should be taken by young folks who have the correct career background for those positions. Many entry-level jobs that high school graduates could easily learn are only open to college graduates, even though nothing they studied in college has any relevance to the work they are doing.

How did we ever arrive at the point where we are pressuring *all* students to take courses that emphasize abstract liberal arts and ignore practical boots on the ground learning?

I found this blog by Michael J. Petrilli on *Flypaper,* which is part of the Thomas B. Fordham Institute. This fellow makes a lot of sense. "What if our own paper-credentialed life experiences and ideologies are blinding us to alternative pathways to the middle class — including some that might be a lot more viable for a great many young people? Asking all students to pass Algebra II makes a lot of sense if you expect all of them to go to college. But when you are willing to acknowledge that that's a fools errand, you start to see such mandates as barriers to opportunity — the opportunity to pursue career and technical programs that are likely to produce better long-term outcomes for young people." Michael J Petrelli, "College Is Not For Everyone. Let's Stop Pretending it is." *Flypaper*, March 20, 2014.

Hmm.

Our present approach is clearly discriminatory, especially against the large number of students such as Emily, who have skills in spatial and applied areas and who are losers in the job market. But it also discriminates against the top academic 30% such as Jaylen, who could be outstanding college students — assuming they have the desire and determination to do so. A comparison to the military makes me think of the Navy Seals and other elite military units. They are special because they are highly selective, have clear goals, and undergo rigorous training.

Today, academic preparation for many college-bound students is not sufficiently demanding in middle school or high school, and they are not competing against top academic students when they reach the college level. As a result, they learn to slide by — if they make it to college. And we may be losing a whole cadre of gifted students.

It's time to think about our goals and reorganize education in ways that benefit the student and not well-meaning politicians and administrators. Again, neuroscience teaches us that not every person is a left-brainer who is more comfortable with abstract verbal reasoning, as opposed to the right-brainer who is more comfortable with visual, physical, and creative activities. Not every child has the academic brainpower, motivation, ability to focus, and self-control, to achieve at a university level, and not every child has the creative brainpower, motivation, and self-control to succeed in *advanced* career studies.

Good politics.
Some politicians seem to be catching on and responding in a way that will help our students. State Sen. Don Gaetz has led efforts in Florida to increase career opportunities. His Senate Bill 850, which was enacted into law in 2014, makes Cape Digital Tool search certificates and Cape Industry Certifications available to students, including students with disabilities, in prekindergarten through grade 12. This is a step in the right direction and Sen. Gaetz deserves much praise for his long-standing efforts to energize our current educational system. *www. flsenate.gov.*

State Representative Brian Nelson introduced legislation in 2011 to establish a career-oriented path to high school graduation. "Florida Teens Education Bills Taking Shape Ahead of Legislative Session," Jeffrey S. Solochek, *Saint Petersburg Times*, September 3, 2011.

Unfortunately, Nelson's bill couldn't fend off the state achievement testing that is required for every child and that drives our kids into what I term the killing fields.

Advanced technical education can't wait until graduation from senior high school or entry into a community college. These students will have already given up, and the required academic courses may actually interfere with their ability to focus on technical areas. Students will continue to drop out, and the mishmash of career kids and academics will continue to frustrate the majority of students and their teachers.

The enlightened superintendent of schools in Pinellas County, Florida, has recommended replacing two closed schools with new magnet schools as model schools of technology *for elementary students*. At the same time, his school district hopes to introduce rigorous academic models with a global flavor, including pre-Cambridge studies and the International Baccalaureate program at *elementary and middle grades*.

These educational innovations, designed to help public schools compete with charters and private schools, are already moving in the direction proposed by this book. These few magnet schools draw parents and students from all over the county, but waiting lists are long. Lisa Gartner, "Closed schools May Get New Life," *Tampa Bay Times*, December 10, 2013. Cara Fitzpatrick, "Schools to Offer More Options," *Tampa Bay Times*, December 25, 2013.

They are positive steps for both AAS and ACS students, but retain the stubborn *selective* aspects that leave many students behind. They also still retain state achievement test requirements for ACS students that consume valuable time and effort, and restrict their entry to career education.

This gives our elephant heartburn and makes her want to sit on a few government folks!

One program that has managed to avoid the selective aspects of magnets, fundamental schools, and charters, is Clearwater High School in Clearwater, Florida (a school I mentioned earlier). All incoming ninth graders are helped to choose one of four career academies. These academies include business, aerospace, fine arts and sports hospitality. As a result, this wall-to-wall high school has a 100% enrollment in career academies. Each academy also includes core academic teachers. Unfortunately, the state still requires high-stakes testing and has even reduced test credits given for career work.

Rather than a smorgasbord approach, the elephant's plan will offer an introduction to academic and career programs in elementary and middle school, followed by full-blown career and collegiate options at the high school level. And it won't require full-time career kids to suffer through state academic tests in order to earn nationally approved certifications, or college prep kids to make a hammer in less than four hours in order to qualify for advanced trigonometry.

Naysayers.
Which groups will oppose reforming a system that tramples on both academic types and career types? You might think it would be African-Americans and other minority groups — and you could well be correct. That was the case 40 years ago when I was asked to consult with a committee of well-intended public school teachers and administrators. We thought it would help students with little academic interest to provide vocational programs. But the offerings at that time were nothing like the exciting and interesting career programs now available.

Black parents worried that many of the youngsters channeled out of the mainstream would be African-American students and other minorities, along with kids from lower socio-economic backgrounds. They were fearful that the proposed program was nothing more than a not-so-subtle form of segregation and discrimination, because the technical programs were quite limited.

Today, minority groups seem more open to recognizing individual differences. They register their children for special magnet programs and tolerate full-blown IQ evaluations to determine if their children meet the cutoff for gifted programs. Adjustments have been made to allow participation at somewhat lower IQ levels for children from minority and disadvantaged backgrounds — but there is still a cut-off that is based on IQ testing.

They also realize that the present system isn't able to do much for their children. "For years advocates have called for an end to the so-called 'school to prison pipeline,' a nationwide trend that funnels children into the criminal justice system for minor offenses." Zack Peterson, "Disciplining Of Black Students Questioned," *Tampa Bay Times*, June 30, 2014. With the elephant-in-the-classroom approach, all students, White and minority, will have an opportunity to engage in interesting and financially rewarding career studies, even if they come from poor neighborhoods.

This discussion reminds me of England, where I operated a special education program for more than 25 years. Beginning in 1950, British students took comprehensive exams called O levels, and depending on their test score would either go to a tiny number of elite universities such as Oxford and Cambridge or be faced with limited alternatives. I opposed this program because it limited college academics to a tiny fraction of the population and career alternatives were minimal (our elephant, tusk-tusk, recalled her life in the British colonies and didn't want any part of that particular program, either).

Universities.
Ironically, some universities might not be happy because the flow of non-qualified students would slow down. At the present time, many colleges provide extensive remedial training for the students who should probably not be there. These remedial efforts bring additional funds to the colleges and help fill their dormitories.

In an interview with Jon Reynolds, former superintendent of two school districts in the state of Michigan, he reported that when a prestigious state university began expanding dormitory space they dropped the admissions grade-point average from a 3.5 to a 2.7. The Elephant-in-the-Classroom would give universities the type of student they want and complain they don't have — but I'm not sure they will be entirely happy with fewer students.

Support for Dr. Reynolds's comments is found in an article in the *New York Times Magazine* reporting that fully half of our college students from wealthier families can graduate by age 24 even with an SAT score of only 900. Converting test score to percentiles means that these students had math scores placing them at only the 29th percentile. Yes, 29th percentile; not 70th-90th percentile. Paul Tough, "Am I supposed to be here? Am I good enough?" *The New York Times*, May 18, 2014.

Surprisingly, another group that might object to our elephant is White suburban parents and parents from more privileged urban schools. They think the new Common Core Curriculum is toughening up some of the curricula and the testing that goes with it. According to Dana Goldstein, a Schwartz Fellow at the New America Foundation, these parents are leading a *Standardized Test Opt-Out Movement,* which advocates that parents prevent their kids from taking a new generation of tougher exams.

I wonder if these folks are caught up in the "graduate from college or become a lifetime failure" myth. The counter to this argument is Diane Ravitch's opinion that aspects of the Common Core Benchmarks themselves are the problem.

Dana Goldstein interviewed a young woman who wanted to study nursing but still lacked a high school diploma 18 months after the end of her senior year because she failed a global history exam 11 times. Today, some reformers are pushing for *single college and career ready standards for all teens*. Dana Goldstein, "On School Testing, Opt for Tough but Flexible," *Tampa Bay Times*, December 2, 2013. So it's a one track education, regardless of whether they want to attend nursing school or Harvard!

The concept of a single standard for all teens is the total opposite of ideas put forth in this book, and is yet another attempt to force blinders on teachers, students, and school administrators so that we can't see the elephant. A single standard sounds wonderful. Recall my earlier comments about that great American myth, that everyone is the same. In my opinion, this is political posturing or simply reflects ignorance of brain function and individual personality differences. I believe it's repeating the same old mistakes.

What do parents want?

Terry Boehm, Director of the Florida Educational Foundation in St. Petersburg, Florida, told me that feedback sessions show 93% of parents believe that their children will go to college. Forty percent think their kids should have master's degrees! Countering this ingrained attitude will require a multilayered marketing program.

What else do we need to do? First, we need to recognize the elephant. Second, we need state legislatures and local school districts to pass the laws and make the adjustments necessary to ride the elephant for a few years. We've been doing the wrong thing harder, but we are taking tentative steps in the right direction — now we need to do the right thing harder!

The private sector needs to stand up and contribute money as well as personnel. This sector needs to lead the way in raising money, privately and publicly. Equally important is the need to provide apprenticeships and curriculum materials compatible with the workplace.

This sector also needs to hire well-trained, non-college graduates. An example is the fact that there is a pilot shortage in the U.S. right now. One solution may be to hire pilots who are not college graduates. Barry Palmer reported that he was in a class of 25 new pilots and only one had a college education. All completed 25 to 35 years of accident free flying. "Letters to the Editor," *The Wall Street Journal*, February 15 – 16, 2014.

Politicians at the local, state and national level need to get behind this approach. The cry "college for everyone!" is tempting to anyone running for office. But it is time to put the public good first. And the well-being of individual students such as Emily and Jaylen.

Primary thrust.
The primary thrust of this book is to get students such as Emily out of the killing fields and into relevant, productive, career education. The present system is discriminatory because the majority of America's students are denied an education that teaches the skills and employment opportunities they want. It is a system that results in economic inequality. The elephant's plan will eventually close the employment gap, especially for minorities.

State attorneys-general need to recognize the *disparate impact* caused by a system that discourages much-needed career education under the guise of helping students to reach their (college) potential.

There has been much talk of "a war on poverty," but meanwhile our educational system continues to create poverty. The best way to win this war, as with any war, is prevention. Let's stop talking about a war on poverty and win it in the trenches. Let's stop General Lee's ill-fated plan to charge up Cemetery Ridge.

And we need a career system that is not just for the top career students. We must have a system that gives all career students a leg up, even if they can't handle advanced certifications. They can learn basic career specialties and develop the soft skills of cooperation and teamwork that matter so much in today's economy. Our society needs to recognize poverty and encourage opportunity.

Emily and Jaylen.
This story began with the plight of our two fictitious characters, Emily and Jaylen. How would they have fared if the Elephant-in-the-Classroom approach had been available to them? Perhaps they can fill us in.

Jaylen: "I knew the AAS program would be challenging, but my parents believed in me and I graduated with honors. Advanced Placement allowed me to skip several college courses and I graduated in less than four years. I received a scholarship from the Duke University Law School, and I'm presently an elected state representative working to improve my community and state."

Emily: "My mom and I decided to opt for ACS while I was still in seventh grade. I've never been sorry for that decision. I thought I wanted to be a veterinarian assistant but discovered a new talent — welding. My national certifications gave me a job doing welding on skyscrapers. After a couple of years I was making $50,000 year. I'm still single but look forward to marriage and children. Right now, I'm living with my mom and trying to help her out. She's always been there for me."

America, land of enormous charity, freedom, and bravery.
But also a society stuck on the idea that when it comes to education, one-size-fits-all. We are forcing all students to search for a future somewhere in the stratosphere instead of recognizing differing abilities, motivations, and skills. We still believe all people are the same and college is the *only* pathway to a good life.

Nonsense!

Thank you for accompanying me on this journey into the killing fields. Emily, Jaylen, and our sympathetic and now visible elephant are also grateful.

END

To Contact the Author

Mack R. Hicks, Ph.D. founded Center Academy Schools in Atlanta, Georgia, and major metropolitan cities in Florida. He founded the first school in England for children with learning disabilities and attention deficit disorder, and he is a member of the Royal Society of Arts and Commerce. He was a lead scientist on a research grant sponsored by the National Institutes of Mental Health, co-author of *Parent, Child and Community*, Nelson Hall, Chicago, and author of *The Digital Pandemic,* New Horizon Press. His articles can be found on the *Psychology Today Magazine* website where he is a regular contributor, and on his own website, **mack-hicks.com**. Or join him on *Twitter* and *Face Book*.

appendix 1

Crisis in American Education.

Chapter 6 was just too long (and perhaps boring) for right-brainers. As a result, it was shortened. Here are deleted citations:

- Hoping for a return of manufacturing jobs for less skilled workers may be a false hope. While youth unemployment is 14%, Silicon Valley companies and others across the country report that many tech jobs go unfulfilled because applicants lack STEM capabilities (science, technology, engineering and math). Mortimer Zuckerman, Chairman and Editor-in-Chief of *U.S. News &World Report*, "Fight Inequality with Better Jobs," *The Wall Street Journal,* March 3, 2014.

- Teen pregnancy remains a concern. "It takes a big toll. Every adolescent who gets pregnant is a hit on growth for herself, for her community and her country," says Babatunde Osotinehim, Executive Director of the United Nations Population Fund (UNFPA).

- Most people agree that these problems are worsened by our current educational strategies — or lack thereof. According to Rex Tillerson, the US military is forced to turn away applicants because of a lack of preparation in math, science, and other subjects. Each year, approximately 30% of high school graduates who take the Armed Forces Entrance Exam fail the test.

- Are our students ready for college? In 2011, the Scholastic Aptitude Tests showed that reading and writing scores were the lowest ever recorded. The ACT college entrance exam suggested that only 25% of high school graduates were ready for college. Stephanie Banchero, "SAT Reading, Writing Scores Hit Low," *The Wall Street Journal*, September 15, 2011

- In one high school in Florida, the principal has resorted to having recent graduates talk to students about college, the military, and *even the workforce*. (Author emphasis). "Dropping Out Harder To Do," Lisa Gardner, *Tampa Bay Times*, December 22, 2013.

- And what about those who *are* qualified for college? According to Sidney K Pierce, who has been training university students in science for over 40 years, even most "real science majors, as opposed to students taking "dumbed-down" science majors called things like biomedical science, should be doing something else." Pierce has taught approximately 10,000 undergraduate students and estimates that "no more than a few hundred really stood a chance of doing professional science. Better STEM (science, technology, engineering, and math) training is important," he says, "but merely turning out an inadequate product based mostly on headcount, for a mythical job market, won't do it." *St. Petersburg Times*, November 26, 2011.

- Toughening standards may not be easy. The average Chicago teacher makes $76,000 a year in a city where the average worker makes $47,000 a year. Rising school costs have pushed the Chicago school system deep into the red. Meanwhile, 40% of students drop out and only 8% of 11th graders meet college readiness standards. David Brooks, "Battling the Bloat," *Tampa Bay Times*, September 16, 2012.

- The vital link of education and prosperity is pointed out by Paul E. Peterson and Eric A. Hanusheck, who disparage U.S. test scores in math, contrasting the United States to the greater successes of Korea, Taiwan, Singapore, and Hong Kong. *The Wall Street Journal*, September 19, 2013.

- In November, 2013, a mother in Dade City, Florida, was aghast to find that her son made a D in civics and was still placed on the honor roll. She demanded that something change and the Pasco County, Florida, school system agreed with her. In the future it will require all A's or all A's and B's to make the honor roll. Jeffrey S. Solochek, "Cs Will Keep Students in Pasco Off of Honor Rolls," *Tampa Bay Times*, November 15, 2013.

- **What about college?** A survey of 9000 adults born in the early 1980s shows that 32% of women have received a bachelor's degree by age 27, compared with 24% of men. *U.S. Bureau of Labor Statistics*.

- "You're told that to make it in life you must go to college. You work hard to get there; your parents strain their savings or take out huge loans to pay for it. And you end up learning — not much." "Study Finds Learning Can Stall in College," Associated Press, *Tampa Tribune,* January 19, 2011.

- Richard Arum and Josipa Roksa authored the book *Academically Adrift: Limited Learning on College Campuses.* This study of more than 2,300 college undergraduates found that 45% of students showed no significant improvement in key areas of learning. On average, students experienced only a seven percentage point gain in skills during their first two years in college and a marginal gain in the two years after that. Arum and Roksa's study further showed that after four years, 36% of students did not demonstrate significant improvement. Students who spent more time studying with peers and more time in the Greek system (fraternities and sororities) showed decreased rates of learning.

- Many students, parents, and experts believe that colleges have lowered their standards in order to maintain enrollment. Some have criticized the common practice of having students evaluate their professors because professors may try to buy good evaluations by doling out high grades. "When Students Rate Teachers, Standards Drop." Op-Ed, *The Wall Street Journal*, November 6, 2013.

- "We now have vast numbers of people with college credentials working in jobs that call for no academic preparation. At the same time, because of the emphasis on credentials, employers want applicants to have college degrees even for work that high school students could readily learn." George C. Leef, "Letters to the Editor," *The Wall Street Journal*, November 12, 2012.

- According to Richard Vedder, Director of the Center for College Affordability and Productivity, "30% of the adult population has college degrees, yet the Department of Labor tells us only 20% or so of jobs require college degrees. We have 115,520 janitors in the United States with bachelors' degrees. Why are we encouraging more kids go to college?" Lauren Weber, "Do Too Many People Go to College?" *The Wall Street Journal,* June 25, 2012.

- In Florida efforts have been made to raise the passing rate on the state-mandated high school achievement test (FCAT), but the fear is that thousands of Florida school children will have lower scores. This would open the door for students to use vouchers and transfer from their assigned schools. School officials believe these transfers may be detrimental to the overall student population. "Passing FCAT Scores May Rise," *St. Petersburg Times,* December 9, 2011.

- One week later, the State of Florida admitted that the graduation figures they provide include thousands of struggling students who transferred into adult education programs to earn a GED (High School Graduate Equivalency Diploma). Under the new formula, these GED students would not be included and this would result in a lower graduation rate. "Next year, Florida Won't Be Able to Hide Them." Ron Matus, *St. Petersburg Times*, December 13, 2011.

- The latest scores from NAEP show sluggish improvement in most states. Despite massive efforts to raise math and reading standards in the classroom and evaluate teachers through student testing, only small gains have been seen. Stephanie Banchero, "Test Scores Show Small Gains," *The Wall Street Journal,* November 8, 2013.

- **Common Core.** All of these problems affect colleges and their graduates. Secretary of Education Arnie Duncan has proposed that colleges be measured by the gainful employment of the graduates and repayment of federal loans. But this could encourage universities to admit fewer students from low income backgrounds that must finance their education. The more the student borrows, the lower the score the university would receive from the federal government.

- According to David Leonhardt, only 44% of low-income high school seniors with high standardized test scores enroll in a four year college. David Leonhardt, *The New York Times*, May 30, 2011.

- **Community colleges?** Only 30% of students enrolled in community colleges nationwide complete their associate's degree on time — or even graduate. *Tampa Bay Times*, April 19, 2019.

appendix 2

Career Offerings.

Here are examples of the kinds of career activities that should be made available to all students.

Courses available at the Center for Advanced Technologies in Pinellas County, Florida: This is a high school program, 9th through 12th grades. Offerings include art, digital video and sound fundamentals, cyber security, debate, environmental science, introduction to information technology, science, musical theater, medical skills, new media, newspaper research, robotics, sculpture, stagecraft, and team sports.

Here are courses from the Pinellas County Technical Education Centers, which are separate from regular high school technical programs: professional development, office, health services, childcare recertification, intuit quick books certification, air-conditioning, refrigeration, heating technology, business ethics, education skills, customer service, commercial vehicle driving, heating, ventilation, air-conditioning, and practical nursing.

The St. Petersburg Community College offers a choice of certifications. One can obtain a certificate in accounting applications, business, industry, entrepreneurship, international business, management, leadership, marketing, sign language interpretation, computer support, Cisco network, Linux system administrator, Microsoft certified server, computer programming specialist certificate, Java certificate, mobile device certificate, open-source certificate, visual basic net certificate, information technology certificate, drafting certificate.

Computer aided design and drafting certificate, engineering, technology support certificate, greenbelt certificate, medical quality system certificate, rapid prototyping certificate, food and beverage management certificate, computer related crime investigation certificate, homeland security certificate, crime scene technology certificate, emergency management certificate, fire investigator certificate and fire officer certificate.

This community college also offers many associate degrees and bachelor's degrees. According to the Georgetown University Center on Education and the Workforce, average wages for graduates of a community college in Tennessee is $1300 higher than average salaries for graduates of the state's four-year institutions.

Here are some associate degree programs: computer networking degree, technology management degree, web development degree, early childhood education degree, aviation maintenance technology degree, architectural design and construction, drafting and design technology, engineering technology and digital arts, media and interactive web design, music industry, recording arts degree, photographic technology degree, dental hygiene degree, paramedic degree, funeral services degree, health information technology degree, alcohol and substance abuse degree, social services degree, physical therapist assistant degree, radiography degree, hospitality and tourism management degree, environmental science technology degree, nursing degree, paralegal studies degree, criminal justice degree, crime scene technology degree, fire science technology, etc.

Wow!

appendix 3

The Career Test.

This is not a scientific "test" based on research with representative samples from across the country. Let's just call it the author's informal checklist or inventory. This list might be helpful to parents and students who are thinking about career studies.

This student:
1. Falls below the 70th percentile (60th percentile if free or reduced lunch student) on national or state norm-referenced achievement tests at the end of the eighth grade? Yes = 65 points
2. OR below the 50th percentile? Yes = 75 points
3. Feigns illness before big tests? Yes = 10 points
4. Creative, but easily bored? Yes = 10 points
5. Frequently talks of dropping out of school Yes = 10 points
6. Enjoys fixing or building things? Yes = 20 points
7. Can't study for more than 30 minutes at one time Yes = 20 points
8. Rarely reads for enjoyment? Yes = 20 points
9. Dislikes phonics and/or spelling? Yes = 10 points
10. Often loses books and or homework? Yes = 10 oints
11. Poor attention span? Yes = 15 points
12. Can't delay, must do it now!? Yes = 15 points
13. Has never liked school much? Yes= 15 points
14. Gets Ds and Fs on essays and reports? Yes= 20 points

15. Grade point average of 3.0 or below? Yes= 25 points
16. Says school is boring? Yes= 15 points

While this is not a rigorous, standardized survey, a minimum score of 100 would indicate a desirable path toward advanced career studies (ACS).

appendix 4

The College Test.

This is not a scientific "test" based on research with representative samples from across the country. Let's just call it the author's informal checklist or inventory. This list might be helpful to parents and students who are thinking about advanced academic studies (AAS).

Does this student:
1. Fall in the top 30% in overall achievement (top 40% for free-lunch students) compared with other students completing the eighth grade on a norm-referenced standardized test, comparing the student with all students across the country; not just the students in his or her school?   Yes = 35 points
2. *Or* if falls in top 10% on these tests?   Yes = 60 points
4. Above average middle-school grades?   Yes = 35 points
5. Is a good test taker?   Yes = 10 points
6. Reads at least 5 books per year?   Yes = 10 points
7. Finds classes interesting?   Yes = 5 points
8. Talks about favorite teachers?   Yes = 10 points
9. Discusses world events with friends?   Yes = 10 points
10. Can study without interruption for two + hours?   Yes = 15 points
11. Wants to get good grades?   Yes = 5 points
12. Enjoys school social activities?   Yes = 5 points

13. Gets mostly A's on written essays? Yes = 10 points
14. Willing to pay $120,000: loans for tuition, ($30,000), and the cost of leaving the workforce for 4-5 years? Yes = 10 points

While this is not a rigorous, standardized survey, a minimum score of 100 would indicate a reasonable path toward advanced academic studies (AAS) and college.

appendix 5

Non-College Grads.

When Oprah Winfrey didn't complete college her father stayed on her to finish. "He'd say, 'Oprah Gail — I don't know what you're gonna do without that degree.' And I'd say, 'But dad, I have my own television show.' And he'd say, 'Well, I still don't know what you're going to do without that degree.'" "Blackboard — Quoted," *The New York Times*, April 13, 2014.

Yes, the pressure is on. Everyone in America goes to college! But we know better, don't we? And you don't have to be a high-flying celebrity making millions of dollars to succeed outside of college. Industrious people from all walks of life have done very well, not just financially, but also in terms of living happy, productive, and honorable lives.

Matt Thompson is one of those people. My wife and I met Matt at the upscale Customs House Resort in Boston. Matt was one of the managers, and we were impressed with his intelligence and positive outlook. When I asked Matt where he went to college, he paused for a second or two before replying — he wasn't a college graduate.

A few weeks later, Matt and I talked on the phone. He reported that he began questioning the value of academics while still in high school. He held part-time jobs and really enjoyed meeting a variety of people. He also believed that much of what he was learning in school was "out of touch with reality and disconnected from the world." He started to correct some of his teachers' opinions, which wasn't appreciated, and he often felt out of step.

His father was university graduate and wanted Matt to go to college. Matt entered college and was getting straight A's. By the end of his freshman year he was feeling, along with his classmates, that he was "cool" and superior to those who didn't attend college. He worked part-time at a warehouse and once again enjoyed interacting with "real" people. Matt then worked part-time at a sporting goods outlet and noticed that some of the college-graduate managers were ill-equipped to do their jobs.

Matt was too young to become a manager and decided to leave the sporting goods store to pursue a new career path. He was attending school part time at this point. He applied to the Marriott Corporation and was given a job as a front desk clerk. From there he worked his way up to become a supervisor, and at the age of 21 became a manager of a Marriott Courtyard Hotel. Since then he has held five management positions with Marriot.

Matt is doing well financially and is proud of his solid knowledge base. He is pleased with the fact that he saved lots of money by not continuing college for three more years and, as a result, had no college debt. He believes in being fiscally responsible and says "the best way to give yourself a raise is to cut your expenditures." He reads voraciously and has an active social life. When asked if friends criticize him for not being a college graduate, he said they don't, but on rare occasions when his lack of a college degree comes up in conversation, " it takes the air out of the room."

He has no plans to attend college or to take online courses to obtain what he thinks of as a bogus piece of paper. He's proud of his independence and would like to help others see the benefits of a challenging life in the real world — outside of college. He refers to Martin Luther King when he says that a person should be judged by his heart and not his skin or his pedigree.

Matt Thompson, another American who didn't fulfill the American dream of graduating from college. Another person who doesn't respond to a common core because he thinks that there is nothing common about himself or others. This country could use a lot more like him.

appendix 6

Help Your Child — Now!

What to do now.
If you agree with the Elephant-in-the-Classroom approach, you'll want to contact your school board representatives and legislators. Let them know if you believe your child is trapped in the killing fields. Ask for access to advanced career studies or advanced academic studies, depending on your child's special attributes and abilities. Ask them to read this book. If change won't come in time to help your child, what should you do?

Sign up.
Contact your school board and politely inquire about all new and existing *selective* programs in your county. These may be special schools that are separate from your neighborhood school, including magnets, fundamental schools, or wall-to-wall career schools. Or they could be special programs within your neighborhood school. Look into charters (no cost privately-operated public schools) that have a good reputation and inquire with private schools about state-supported vouchers, personal learning accounts, or educational savings accounts, that you could use to enroll your child in a private school.

You need to get savvy about your school district's culture of diverse and changing programs. People at the school board will help you. These are good people who will be happy to give you information about public school programs.

The key.
The key is to know about all these programs in advance so that you can be first in line to sign up your child. You'll want your child in a highly selective school, one that has a waiting list — the longer the better. It's less important to match

your child with the advertised and narrowly-defined program at the selective school than it is to escape the killing fields and have your child in a stable environment where other parents care enough to research their child's school or program and are willing to study and stand in line to get their child in. These schools may offer advanced career studies or advanced academic studies.

You need to get on mailing lists so that you will know what's coming. These programs are often reviewed in the newspaper once or twice a year, but you need to know about them in advance and get your child signed up. What if your child is interested in learning Chinese, but a highly selective school emphasizes communications? Go with the most selective public school you can find. If a highly selective school program matches your child's interests, all the better. But the main thing is to get into an environment that is safe and secure and where teachers and parents are united in their goal to teach your child SOMETHING. ANYTHING!

If the special school says your child must be interested in political science to obtain admission, get interested in political science, pronto! I know that this is contrary to the main premise of this book. We want to match children's personalities and abilities to their education. But this is an emergency solution until things change for the better. And don't forget that there is a 70% chance that your child should enter career studies rather than college prep courses. Don't fall for the myth that every child must go to college and don't worry about neighbors or friends who still subscribe to this myth. Keep your child's happiness and future in mind. Look into career programs, whether in your neighborhood public school or in public school wall-to-wall career academies.

Carrying this over to the college level, I've had parents approach me because a mediocre college with watered-down academics offered stagecraft, which matched their child's interest. But that child was also accepted at a prestigious university. I recommended the highly-rated school because of the overall environment and the contacts that can be made. Stagecraft can be learned later, at special institutes, assuming the child is still committed to that field after exposure to an enormous menu of fascinating and financially rewarding careers.

Foundations.
Contact local private foundations or public school groups that want to increase career offerings and/or toughen up college prep courses. Your state representative and senator need to hear about this, as well as members of your school board. Most of these folks realize this is a shortcoming and want to increase expenditures for programs that work, whether advanced academic studies or advanced career studies.

You may want to consider moving to a different geographical area within your district, one that is located near a top public school. More than two-thirds of adults with children under the age of 12 say the neighborhood school district is among the most important considerations when choosing a home. @jedkolko, *The Atlantic, CITYLAB,* August 13, 2014.

If you are already zoned for an elite public school and your child has all four of the elephant's legs necessary for an authentic college or university, you may be wise to stay where you are. Or, there may be special exceptions that will permit your child to attend a school that your child is not zoned for. I recall a group of parents who discovered that if a foreign language course was not offered in their zoned school, but was offered in another school, they could transfer their child. In this case, the language course that unlocked the door to the elite school was German.

Costs.
Keep finances in mind. If your child is in the top 25-30% of students on a state or nationally-normed achievement test (not the state or federal test used to judge your teacher or school), college may be the right destination for your child, assuming he or she is motivated and has the willpower and ability to focus that are also necessary. This could cost as much as $50,000 in lost earnings while attending college, in addition to the cost of college. Sometimes two years of study at a community college saves on cost.

Don't forget about private tutoring. It may give your child a better chance to get into a selective program, whether that program is academic or career oriented.

About the Author

Dr. Mack R Hicks was trained as a *scientist – practitioner* in clinical programs at the University of Florida in Gainesville, Florida and at the University of Wisconsin in Madison, Wisconsin, where he interned as a psychology fellow in the medical school. This was after receiving a bachelor's degree from the University of Notre Dame.

Hicks had a successful private practice for over 30 years and opened one of the first school programs in the United States for children with learning disabilities. At the present time he is president of the board of 12 *Center Academy Schools*. He founded the first school for dyslexic and ADHD children in the United Kingdom. As a result, Dr. Hicks became a Fellow of the Royal Society of Arts and Commerce.

He wrote the first state-wide voucher legislation (SB 420) in the United States, a pilot scholarship program designed to cover five Florida counties, providing for educational vouchers for children enrolled in the free lunch program. It was the first voucher bill to make its way through the Florida Senate Education Committee and onto the floor of the State Senate.

Dr. Hicks had weekly radio programs in child development on WBVM, covering Florida's West Coast. He is a regular contributor to the *Psychology Today Magazine* website. He has written journal articles and books about child development and learning.

Additional information regarding his work can be found at his website, **mack–hicks.com** — and on Twitter.

www.ingramcontent.com/pod-product-compliance
Lightning Source LLC
Chambersburg PA
CBHW031356040426
42444CB00005B/319